Testimonials

"With his concept of Spirit Whisperers, Chick Moorman gives
us a way to remember that in this time of high-stakes
testing, national standards, and accountability in schools, those
of us who can connect with the human side of learning give
students what they need the most."

Kenneth R. Freeston, Superintendent
The public schools of Easton, Redding and Region No. 9
Monroe, CT

"Uplifting, inspiring, and encouraging. I feel validated and
affirmed. Thank you for sharing this important message."

Kathleen A. Nace
High school teacher
Hampton, NJ

"Is there any way this could be made required reading for those
thinking about entering the field of education?"

Dr. Bob Roden, Assistant Superintendent
Stark County Education Service Center
Canton, OH

"I wish every teacher would read this book. There is something
here for every one of us. This book is a wonderful guide on how
to unleash the power that is within each of us to be a
Spirit Whisperer. Definitely a teachers' tool."

Sandra L. Darling, Instructor
New Hampshire Technical College

"Eye-opening and heartwarming. A how-to book for teachers who want to teach to a child's spirit."

Rev. Neltje Marie Brawer
Kalamazoo, MI

"Thanks for reminding the Spirit Whisperers within us that there is so much more to education than scores, assessments, and standardized tests!"

Mimi Brodsky Chenfeld
Author of *Teaching Is the Key of Life*
Columbus, OH

"Spirit Whisperers is an affirmation of all that is right in education. This inspiring text will serve to encourage new teachers and recognize those dedicated educators who have given so much so that their students could discover and develop their potential. I am excited to share this delightful book with my colleagues."

Sarah Knapp, M.S.W.
School social worker and parenting consultant
Grand Rapids, MI

"In this day and age of increased diversity in classrooms, this book is a necessity. Thank you for putting the spirit back in 'mind, body, and spirit.'"

Mary Montle Bacon, Ph.D.
Psychologist
Hillsborough, CA

Spirit Whisperers
Teachers Who Nurture a Child's Spirit

CHICK MOORMAN

Personal Power Press
Merrill, MI

SPIRIT WHISPERERS:
Teachers Who Nurture a Child's Spirit

©2001 by Chick Moorman and Personal Power Press

Library of Congress Catalogue
Card Number 00 093527   ISBN   0-9616046-5-4

Printed in the United States of America

Personal Power Press
P.O. Box 547
Merrill, MI 48637

Cover Design:
Foster & Foster, Inc.—www.fostercovers.com

Book Design:
Tagline Communications, Inc.—www.taglineinc.com

Dedication

For my grandchildren,
Chelsea, Austin, and Olivia.
May all their teachers be Spirit Whisperers.

TABLE OF CONTENTS

Preface

The purpose of this book is to honor and encourage the Spirit Whisperer that exists within every person working with young people today.

Spirit Whisperers exist. They are out there in every school, in every grade level, in every part of the country. They coach, they lead youth groups, they teach school, they counsel, they administer, and they parent. Most often they do their work in anonymity. Quietly, steadily, they go about their task of teaching to a child's spirit. This book is an effort to celebrate Spirit Whisperers and help them remember that there are others like them who are working to inspire, nurture, uplift, and help young people tune in to the spirit and power within.

Spirit Whisperers are "way showers." They show us that education can be much more than ranking, rating, and judging our unique children. They remind us that shame-based, right/wrong, competitive doctrines do not work in today's schools and are not working in our society. They help us see that the test makers have shaped their tests and now the tests are shaping us, determining much of what we value as educators and citizens. They help us stay conscious of the notion that real education has nothing to do with covering content. Education is now and has always been a drawing out of what already exists within the student rather than a putting in of what we see as necessary to fill perceived deficiencies.

Spirit Whisperers give us hope. They help us create a vision of an educational system that doesn't perceive failure, that grants dignity without it needing to be earned, that recognizes punishment as serving the needs of the punishing adult rather than those of the student, that holds the child in a state of grace, even as appropriate consequences are implemented. They help us see the value of treating every child as special without the limiting beliefs of "best" and "better." Spirit Whisperers help us lift our eyes, our hearts, and our spirits to see and remember again what is possible when the main purpose of education becomes the creation of who and what we choose to be.

This book is about the new curriculum, the silent curriculum, the curriculum that Spirit Whisperers are implementing day after day in their classrooms, churches, and meeting rooms. That curriculum is more process-centered than concerned with end products. It helps young people learn to be solution-oriented, self-responsible, personally empowered, self-expressing, and free. It deals with concepts of respect, honesty, sharing, acceptance, awareness, integrity, forgiveness, and love.

The new curriculum demonstrates that being right doesn't work, that we are all connected, that all behavior equals a choice, and that "I am" is more important than I.Q. It allows students to learn that being is as important as doing, more is not necessarily better, and there is no one best way. It gives opportunities for students to practice looking within for answers and to learn that perception is a choice.

This book is a celebration of Spirit Whisperers. It is intended to encourage them to pat themselves on the back and to continue to be light bearers, those who shine light on others whose spirit is covered with layers of illusion and fear. It is also intended to provide ideas and techniques that will empower Spirit Whisperers and enable them to bring more light to the youngsters they love and serve.

All of the names in this book are fictitious, although the events and the examples are real, drawn from incidents I have seen or have been told about at workshops or in schools. They are real stories from real people who work with real students. On occasion, I have combined more than one incident into one concise example.

I wish to thank every teacher, too numerous to mention, who sent me ideas, thoughts, and encouragement as I worked on this manuscript. A special thank you to those individuals who read and reread my writings and offered their heartfelt suggestions. They include John Schmitt, Rick Benedict, Steve Barkley, Miriam Georg, Steve Shekell, Sarah Knapp, and Tom and Valerie Haller. Nancy Lewis, as she has done with my two previous books, made an enormous contribution with her editing skills and helpful suggestions.

It is no accident that you hold this book in your hands at this time. It may be that when the book is ready, the reader appears. It may also be that when the reader is ready, the book appears. It doesn't matter; either way we are connected. Thank you for being ready. Thank you for helping bring this book into existence. Thank you for attracting it into your life and thus into the lives of the young people with whom you share.

I envision a day when there are no more Spirit Whisperers, only Spirit Shouters. Together we can bring that day closer. Let's not *do* it. Let's *be* it.

Chick Moorman

Introduction

A Spirit Whisperer could be any teacher, parent, para-educator, administrator, coach, counselor, bus driver, secretary, lunchroom aide, or grandparent. He could be present in a child's life short-term or be there on a permanent basis. He might teach down the hall or live next door. You could even be a Spirit Whisperer yourself.

A Spirit Whisperer is any adult who teaches to a child's spirit. She believes that to teach effectively she must address the entire trilogy of a child's mind, body, and spirit. She stays conscious of the fact that in our current educational system the portion of that trio that is most often neglected is the third part—spirit.

Spirit Whisperers care more about a student's attitude and energy than they do about his ability to memorize. A student's sense of personal power, degree of belief in herself, and level of personal responsibility command more of a Spirit Whisperer's attention than facts and reasons for historical events. Spirit Whisperers care more deeply about helping children acquire a spirit of inquiry and a zest for life than they do about the accumulation of answers to trivia questions. Helping students develop an appreciation of diversity and an understanding of the concepts of self-responsibility, integrity, self-expression, awareness, oneness, and conscious creation become the tenets of a Spirit Whisperer's mission.

The following scenario illustrates the essence of a Spirit Whisperer. The day it occurred was not among my favorites. It involved attending the funeral and reception for Bill, a former colleague and friend who had died unexpectedly in what seemed like the prime of his life. I wanted to be there, and I didn't want to be there. My desire was to say goodbye to Bill one final time and be supportive of his family and other colleagues, but my attendance felt more like an obligation than an uplifting way to spend an afternoon.

I dressed slowly, thinking of this 15-year teaching veteran. He had taught math in the high school and coached the boy's basketball team. He had served on the negotiating committee and took his professional practice seriously.

As I drove from the funeral to the reception, I noticed I was in a slight depression. My head was down as I walked up the sidewalk to the hall the family had rented for the event. That decision turned out to be a wise one. An inordinate number of people showed up—more than would normally be expected at an event of this nature. Friends, relatives, colleagues, and students attended to pay their last respects. Many of Bill's current students were present. So were former students, representing this man's entire teaching career.

As I moved into the crowd I acknowledged acquaintances politely, but I didn't feel like talking. Food was in abundance, but I didn't feel like eating. I found a chair in the corner and slumped into it. From that perch I watched and listened, and I confirmed what I already suspected. Bill had been a Spirit Whisperer.

From my spot in the corner I began to eavesdrop. I sat and listened as many of Bill's current and former students discussed the impact he had and was still having on their lives. The comments I was hearing moved me emotionally. They also moved me physically and I began to walk around the room to gain a wider perspective and to grasp more clearly the flavor of the conversations. Not trusting my memory, and knowing I was hearing something important, I recorded what I overheard on the only recording material I could find—napkins.

What I heard was indeed impressive. What I didn't hear was equally impressive. I heard no one say, "He was a good math teacher. He taught me a lot of math." I did hear, "He was a good man. He taught me to believe in myself."

Not one former student who came to honor my friend that day said, "He helped me learn about ratio and isosceles triangles." Someone did say, "He taught me I could do anything I set my mind on."

A 19-year-old college student remarked, "He saw in me something I didn't see in myself at the time. He helped me look at that and acknowledge it." No one said, "Boy, I sure learned a lot of chapter terms from that guy."

No one said, "Man, could he ever cover content!" But I heard a recent college graduate remark, " He helped me learn to look within for my own answers. Remember how he used to say, 'The important answers aren't in the book. They're within you?'" One young woman, a few years out of school, remarked, "What I learned from him was that all conditions are temporary. How they change depends on me."

Nobody said, "He taught me how to sink free throws and play defense." What I did hear was, "He taught me that ethics are more important than rules. What I learned from him is that integrity is a choice I make. He was a wonderful coach."

Not one athlete commented on the number of games they had won. And most of them had won a lot of games. But one former basketball player remarked, "He taught me to take pride in wearing the uniform. I think he'd like to know I still show that same pride today with my business suit."

My friend was truly a Spirit Whisperer. The evidence is in the legacy he left in the hearts and minds of his former students. He touched their spirit and helped them to reach in and touch it as well.

Don't misinterpret what I'm saying here. It's not that Spirit Whisperers don't care about math, history, art, technology, music, language arts, literature, spelling, and music. They do! And they do a good job of teaching the subjects of their choice. It's just that they don't see the delivery of content as their main objective.

Spirit Whisperers do not lose sight of the fact that they are really teaching students to swim. They see math, history, and science as merely the water they are splashing around in. Science teachers let students splash around in science. Literature teachers structure their lessons so their students splash around in literature. Music teachers allow students to get wet with music. It is during the splashing around in the waters of science, math, and music that Spirit Whisperers teach their students to swim.

Don Silvera lets his seventh-graders splash around in social studies and language arts. Like a lot of teachers, Don suffers from insomnia. Oh, he doesn't do it all the time—just when he has students on his mind. You see, with a professional educator like Don, concern for a student tends to get in the way of other activities, particularly a good night's sleep.

This past year Don had good reason to be concerned. Many of his seventh-graders were having trouble reading. Don didn't need achievement tests to confirm what he already knew. These students were reading on a second- or third-grade level. It's a challenge to work with middle school students that are several grade levels behind in any subject. Especially reading.

In addition to the challenge of working with frustrated students, Don was having trouble locating second- and third-grade reading material that looked like it belonged in the middle school. These struggling seventh-graders weren't enjoying having other seventh-graders observe them reading from books that gave the flavor of elementary school. They felt embarrassed and humiliated to be seen with primary materials in their hands.

It was the lack of an immediate solution that produced Don's restless night. The restless night in turn produced the solution. Somewhere in the middle of that space between half-asleep and out like a light, Spirit whispered and the idea came. Trusting Spirit, but not trusting himself to remember the message in the morning, Don got up and wrote the idea down. Before a secure slumber enveloped him that evening, Don added detail to the plan he would begin implementing the next day.

At school the following morning, Don shared his ideas with Lorna, his teaching partner. Lorna added a few ideas of her own, and the result was a full-blown cross-age tutoring program that would send struggling seventh-grade readers a few blocks away to work at an elementary school with struggling second- and third-grade readers.

Twice a week the seventh-graders worked with their assigned reading buddy at the elementary school. During the other school days, they met with Don and Lorna and prepared for upcoming tutoring sessions with the younger students. Preparation required them to bring reading material from the elementary school back to their classroom so they could get ready for the next session. Don's late night idea made it more than legitimate for seventh-graders to be reading third-grade material in a seventh-grade classroom. It made it necessary.

Early in the implementation phase, Don and Lorna could see that the benefits to students would stretch far beyond their initial goal of reading improvement. During the first meeting with the novice tutors, one of the seventh-graders asked, "What do you do when your kid doesn't listen to you?" Don replied, "If you find an effective answer to that one, let me know. I have the same problem with some of my students." Another seventh-grade tutor remarked, "My kid doesn't care. What do you do if your kid doesn't care?" The discussion that followed that inquiry produced insights that influenced students on more than one level.

The cross-age tutoring program turned out to be win/win. Both groups improved their reading skills. Both groups improved their relationship skills. The elementary teachers found a new resource to help them individualize instruction. The young students found a new friend to offer support and encouragement. The seventh-graders found new ways to feel important and successful.

Reading is merely the water these students were splashing around in. It was the medium that allowed the real lessons to come forth: that giving and receiving are connected, and that when we help others, we help ourselves.

Kay Armstrong does her Spirit Whispering in a kinder-garten classroom. She has a required curriculum she is expected to follow. Yet, her understanding of young children, her background in early childhood education, and her commitment to teach to a child's spirit allow her to deviate from that curriculum when she feels it is necessary. She has learned to live *with* it, not *within* it.

Kay and I had been quietly talking about record-keeping procedures for her kindergarten classroom when the buses began to arrive. We noticed the two boys right away. They had begun their altercation sometime before they got to school. Perhaps it had started on the bus. Or maybe it began at the bus stop. It could have been a carryover from the day before. At any rate, it was in full force and totally evident at the time of their arrival.

They burst out of the school bus door pushing, shoving, and proudly proclaiming their existence. We watched as they crossed the grass, mixing threats with gestures and meshing words with actions. By the time the boys reached the schoolroom door, it was clear that words had lost and actions had won. Verbal had given way to physical.

As the youngsters entered the room, they continued their struggle. In an instant they were sprawled on the floor in front of us kicking, slugging, grabbing, squeezing, hanging on, and hollering.

It's times like these that I most appreciate my job. I was the advisor, the visitor. I could enjoy the luxury of being able to sit, observe, and watch a Spirit Whisperer in action. Kay could not. She was the teacher, the person in charge. She had to act.

She went immediately to the boys and separated them with gentle firmness. "I can see you boys are angry," she stated.

The words Kay chose sound so simple that it would be easy to miss their beauty and ignore their depth. But to pass them by without closer examination would be to deny Kay her due as a competent professional, her warmth as a sensitive human being, and her ability to whisper to the spirit of young children.

"I can see you boys are angry." Those were her exact words. No more. No less. But the extent of the message she communicated far exceeded the brevity of her comment. Although her words were, "I can see you boys are angry," her message was, "I recognize your feelings. It looks like anger to me. I see it, I hear it, and I respect it. Your anger is an honest emotion and you are entitled to it. I won't try to deny your anger, change it, or make you wrong for feeling it. It is okay to be angry here."

"I can see you boys are angry," she said. The boys nodded, affirming her observation. Kay then took them both by the hand and led them to the woodworking center. She pulled out a box of scrap lumber, some nails, and two hammers. "Now show me just how angry you are by using these hammers on this wood," she challenged them.

Other children began to wander in, and a few minutes later we noticed that the hammering had ended. The boys had tired of the task and had chosen other activities and feelings to experience. They may have found something new to do together. Perhaps they found separate experiences to enjoy. I don't recall. That's not important anyway.

What is important is that Kay had shown two boys an appropriate way to express their anger. She had shown them that anger in and of itself is not bad, but that some ways of expressing it in this setting were not appropriate. She had provided them with a legitimate channel with which to communicate their feelings.

The boys could now look forward to a happy day at school. Kay could look forward to working with two happy boys. It was a nice ending to the beginning of the day.

Spirit Whisperers believe that the human relationship is more important than the facts imparted. They respect people and they respect curriculum. They perceive value in both. They work at bonding with students because they believe students have to know that *you* care before *they* care what you know.

Two men recently approached the counter at the Secretary of State's office with a gait that revealed enthusiasm and purpose. One was a teenager, the other much older. Father and son, I surmised. Both smiled as they waited for the clerk to move in their direction.

I had come to get a license plate for my new horse trailer. As my request was being handled, I listened and observed as the scene between the clerk and the pair beside me unfolded.

"How can I help you?" the clerk asked.

"This young man has come to register to vote," announced the proud parent.

"No problem," the clerk said. "It's good to have you here. We'll have you in and out in just a few minutes. Won't take long at all."

I watched as the son produced his driver's license and signed the necessary documents. The father's hand on the boy's shoulder and the look in his eyes conveyed the pride he felt this day, helping his son sign on for the opportunity to exercise the responsibility of choosing the men and women that would govern for the next few years. A firm handshake and verbal congratulations brought closure to what was obviously an important experience for both men.

As they walked off, I recalled the lack of ritual and rites of passage we have in our culture, for both young men and women. I made a mental note to add this story to one of my parenting workshops, the one that deals with building family solidarity. I was enjoying a warm feeling in reaction to this scene of male bonding when the newly-registered voter returned for a coat he had forgotten,

"Pretty nice to have a dad that'll share these kinds of experiences with you," I commented, wanting to acknowledge that someone had witnessed and enjoyed their shared voter registration process.

"Oh, that's not my dad," the young man replied. "That's Mr. Ryor, my government teacher. He does this for all of his students who turn eighteen. He makes an appointment with us, drives us over here, and makes sure we get registered. He's been doing it for years."

"He does? How come?" I asked.

"Feels it's his responsibility, I guess. He's a government teacher, you know. We all look forward to it. And we respect him for it. No way I'm not going to vote now."

"Well, congratulations on getting registered," I offered, as this government student turned to leave. "And congratulations," I thought to myself, "for having a Spirit Whisperer for a teacher."

A Spirit Whisperer's primary objective is always development of the student's spirit. They focus on the power of belief, developing an "I can" attitude, creating an internal standard, and teaching and modeling a solution-seeking mindset. They believe that all behavior equals a choice, that being is as important as doing, and that power with is more effective than power over. They set up their classrooms so youngsters can learn that the classroom is more than a place of discovery, it is a place of creation—the creation of who you are as a human being.

Spirit Whisperers don't attract a lot of attention to themselves. They go about the business of teaching to a child's spirit without fanfare. Spirit Whisperers whisper.

Although they are aware that a large portion of our current educational system is not working, Spirit Whisperers rarely take on the system publicly. They do not battle the Board of Education over the increased emphasis on high stakes testing, which tends to drive the curriculum in many school districts today. They focus on uplifting the spirits of their students so that higher quality learning and deeper thinking can rise along with them. At the same time, they work on increasing students' skills because they recognize that when students' skills increase, their spirits often increase as well.

Spirit Whisperers do not complain about the amount of content they are expected to cover, although they often believe that where content is concerned less is more. They acknowledge the incredible advances in technology, science, mathematics, and other disciplines in recent years. But they know that significant growth in a child does not occur because of growth in technology, growth in standards, or growth in curriculum. That kind of growth occurs only when a child has grown in spirit.

Spirit Whisperers don't get caught up in debates over the outdated grading system they're expected to use. They simply continue to teach students to believe in themselves regardless of the grading obstacles that are placed before them.

Spirit Whisperers realize that many educators and legislators in the power structure value a return to "the basics," more of the same style of education that hasn't worked well in the past. They believe that continuing to extend the school year without significantly changing our approach during those added days, raising standards without raising consciousness as to how students develop internal motivation, or mandating programs from above with little or no funding to support them is similar to sticking a burned pizza back in the oven because it didn't smell or look right the first time. Spirit Whisperers don't understand the "It isn't working so let's do more of it" approach to improving education.

Because Spirit Whisperers don't find themselves in the mainstream of educational thought or practice, they often do what they do undercover. Without grade level meetings or committee approval, Spirit Whisperers silently and steadily bring meaningful change to education one child at a time. This change is happening in your city, whether you're aware of it or not. It's happening in your school, even if you don't perceive it. Since you're reading this material, there's a good chance it is currently happening in your classroom.

Spirit Whisperers don't need a committee decision to know that publicly placing a child's name on the chalkboard wounds the spirit. They don't need research validation to know that keeping an entire third-grade class in for recess because two children didn't get ready in time pits one child against another, creating separateness and divisiveness in that classroom. They don't need a teacher's manual to prove to them that students cannot learn responsibility when they are constantly being told what to do.

Spirit Whisperers do not lie or become deceitful about what they do in the classroom. They believe in honest, direct, and open communication. In that regard, Spirit Whisperers stay transparent. Yet, they simply do not attract a lot of attention to themselves, preferring instead to do what they do without major announcements or public celebration. When others ask about activities or intentions, they whisper.

Spirit Whisperers believe that what they advocate and support gives them strength, while what they choose to fight weakens them. Spirit Whisperers support actions, ideas, techniques, strategies that develop the child's spirit. Consequently, that is where they invest their time.

A Spirit Whisperer may use the technique of mental imagery to help students achieve goals and increase retention. Rather than fight attacks by vocal segments of society to remove that valuable strategy from their repertoire, a Spirit Whisperer will attempt to understand the fear that lies under that resistance and refuse to strengthen that fear by fighting it. She will use her energy instead to look for common ground. If required, she will stop asking students to visualize and ask instead that students use their imaginations.

Spirit Whisperers guide their behavior by several underlying principles, referred to in this book as the Six Principles of Spirit Whispering, and a set of Basic Beliefs about children, education, and themselves. The Six Principles of Spirit Whispering make up chapters One through Six. The Basic Beliefs follow.

BASIC BELIEFS OF SPIRIT WHISPERERS

1. ALL BEHAVIOR EQUALS A CHOICE.

Turning a paper in on time is a choice. Turning it in late is a choice. Putting someone down is a choice. Giving them a compliment is a choice. Staying conscious is a choice. Going unconscious is a choice. Choosing the power stance is a choice. Choosing to play from the position of victim is a choice.

Getting papers back to students on time is a choice. Returning those papers to students late is a choice. Adding new activities to your lesson plans is a choice. Doing things the same way you did last year is a choice. Holding students accountable is a choice. Letting them off lightly or pretending not to notice are choices.

2. WE DON'T CONTROL ALL THE EVENTS IN OUR LIVES, BUT WE ALWAYS CONTROL WHO WE CHOOSE TO BE IN RELATION TO THOSE EVENTS.

You can't always control whether or not paint gets spilled in your classroom. You do control how you choose to react to paint being spilled in your classroom. You can't control whether or not an irate parent shows up in your classroom after school next Friday. You can decide which part of you—which personal aspect—you want to activate to deal with that irate parent.

3. SPIRIT WHISPERER ENERGY EXISTS IN EVERY ONE OF US.

We all possess an inner knowing, a wise part within that recognizes what is true for us, what is right for us in each changing circumstance. Character, responsibility, and intelligence already exist in every student. It's our job to pull those attributes out, not attempt to cram them in.

Spirit Whisperer energy exists in every student, every teacher, every parent, and in every one of you reading this book. It's even in everyone you wish would read this book. No one lacks Spirit Whisperer energy. Since it's already inside of us, it is not our job to fill ourselves with it, but to allow it to come out.

4. IT'S ALL PERFECT.

If you have a guest speaker and students act respectfully, it's perfect. If you have a guest speaker and students act disrespectfully, that's perfect, too. Your students are providing you with the perfect data you need to help you create the perfect learning experience or design the perfect debriefing* questions to help them examine the issue of respect and their choices surrounding it.

---

* "Debriefing" is a process through which students learn from an experience by talking and writing about it. The process is described in detail in Chapter 2.

If all of your students pass the chapter test on Westward Expansion, that's perfect. If half your students bomb the test, that too is perfect. You now have the perfect information you need to design the perfect re-teaching of the material, or your students have the perfect logical consequence resulting from their decision concerning amount of time relegated to study.

Spirit Whisperers know that everything that is happening in their classroom and in their life is perfect, even if they can't presently figure out how.

5. BEING IS AS IMPORTANT AS DOING.

If I decide to call a parent concerning a student's behavior, picking up the phone and calling them is what I need to *do*. That becomes my "doing." Just as important to the success of that call is how I choose to *be* when I make the call. That becomes my "being." I could decide to be courteous, tactful, confrontive, empathetic, or thorough. With each choice of how to *be*, I dramatically alter the tone, flavor, and outcome of what I decided to *do*: call a parent.

When I give a Lecture Burst, what students *do* is listen and take notes. What they are doing (listening and taking notes) is greatly affected by how they choose to *be* while they do what they do. They could be energetic, curious, bored, frustrated, interested, or appreciative. Each choice changes the listening/note-taking experience.

6. WISDOM IS APPLIED LEARNING.

Almost every adult has learned about the dangers of smoking; yet many continue to smoke. They do not use their lives to demonstrate their learning. They may have *learned* about the dangers of smoking, but unless they can *apply* that knowledge, they lack wisdom.

Most high school students would likely pass a true/false test on litter. Chances are they could write a decent answer to an essay question on the topic as well. Yet, watch the neighborhood lawns immediately following any high school football game in the country. What do you see? Litter. The learning has not been applied; hence, there is no wisdom.

7. PROCESS IS AS IMPORTANT AS PRODUCT.

If your fifth-grade class has been tracking in mud as they come in from recess, it could be time to call a class meeting. As you lead your students through a solution-seeking process, the end result is important. In the end, you want to reach consensus on a workable solution, one that will eliminate mud being tracked in. Several possible solutions exist.

While creating an end product by finding and implementing a solution satisfies one goal, an equally important goal is to have students learn the process of effective solution seeking. Defining the problem, checking perceptions, brainstorming possibilities, and reaching consensus are all part of the solution-seeking process. Letting students move through a structured search for solutions is as important as any end product that might result from the process.

Knowing that the process is as important as the product frees you up to let go of pushing for a certain solution. Since there is not a certain place where you have to arrive, you can begin to relax. You and your students can enjoy the process.

8. *ATTITUDES ARE MORE EASILY CAUGHT THAN TAUGHT.*

Spirit Whisperers know they can never not model. Students are always watching. Spirit Whisperers show respect in the face of disrespect. They use courteous, polite language. They assert with words that share their thoughts and feelings without attacking the character or personality of the other person. They model the search for solutions rather than use blame and punishment. They listen without interrupting. They start and end on time. Spirit Whisperers let their lives do the teaching.

Spirit Whisperers know that students don't take a year of algebra from Mr. Wilson, or third grade from Miss Hester. They take a year of Mr. Wilson for algebra and a year of Miss Hester for third grade.

9. *YOU NEVER GET THERE.*

"My students are a lot better than before, but they're not quite there yet," a middle school teacher informed me as I began the second of a two-weekend cooperative learning training for educators. She was excited about her students' progress over the month-long implementation period between the two training sessions, but she could see that her students had some distance to go before they "got there."

I broke it to her gently. "You never get there," I told her, with as much compassion as I could muster.

When students learn the interpersonal skill of how to listen without interrupting, they can move on to the skill of disagreeing politely. When they have mastered inviting participation, it could be time to address getting started quickly. Learning to share materials can be followed by other skills that students show they need by the behavior they choose in their groups. If you have eliminated dominators, hitchhikers, criticizers, and surface skimming, perhaps it's time to work on summarizing, paraphrasing, giving descriptive feedback, or ignoring distractions. There is always a new skill, a new level, a new learning that students can grow toward. You never get there.

As Spirit Whisperers grow in their desire and ability to teach to a child's spirit, there comes a time when they begin to think, "Now I've got it." Typically, that moment of "Now I've got it" is accompanied by a realization that there is more to "get." The more you learn, the more you learn there is more to learn. You, as well as your students, never get there.

10. *MORE IS NOT NECESSARILY BETTER.*

More rules, more standards, more content to cover, more time on task, more discipline, more homework, more school days, more in-service, more materials, more parent involvement, more money, more planning time, more cooperation from the administration, more studying, more award assemblies are not necessarily better. More is just more.

Do more standards assure that students develop the intellectual ability and attitude to meet those standards? Do more school days automatically encourage students to use those days to their advantage? Does more discipline help youngsters develop the internal controls necessary to employ self-discipline? Does more time in the oven cure a burned pizza? Does it help to give a dead horse more of the whip?

11. *WHEN THE TEACHER IS READY, THE STUDENT WILL APPEAR.*

Do not confuse this belief with the more popular version, when the student is ready, the teacher will appear, which is used to remind ourselves that when we are ready to learn a particular lesson, a teacher shows up, right on schedule. The belief behind this more popular saying is that the universe doesn't supply the teacher until the readiness level of the student reaches a critical mass. Then, as if on cue, a teacher comes on the scene to deliver the needed or desired lesson.

Spirit Whisperers believe that when the *teacher* is ready, the student will appear. They take the attitude that if a challenging student enters their life and their classroom, that relationship is no accident. They believe they attracted that student into their lives for a reason. Either the universe sees the teacher as ready to cope skillfully with this student, or it is sending the teacher a message that it is time to learn the skills necessary to interact skillfully with this youngster.

Are you experiencing a student who is particularly challenging? If so, it may be helpful to remember that you have drawn this student to you for a reason. It is no accident that you and this student have come together in this space at this time. Your coming together is not some strange coincidence that the masters of fate have randomly dealt you. Regardless of the degree of challenge this student presents, you must be ready, or she wouldn't be presenting herself to you. When the teacher is ready, the student appears.

12. THERE IS NO ONE BEST WAY.

There are many ways to teach reading, many ways to learn long division, many ways to be exposed to *The Canterbury Tales*. In each case, there is no one *best* way. The phonics approach to the teaching of reading may work for one child, while whole language may be the catalyst that springs another child into a lifetime love of the printed word.

Cooperative learning is not the best way for all middle-schoolers to learn. It is merely another way. Lab work is not the best way for every high-schooler to learn science. It is one of many ways that have the potential to be effective.

Better begets best. Best leads to feelings of superiority. Superiority leads to feeling and acting as if you are right.

13. BEING RIGHT DOESN'T WORK.

I'm reminded of the cartoon I saw a few years ago that showed a patient in a hospital bed bandaged from head to toe, with both arms and legs in traction. The doctor stood near the bed looking at her clipboard. The words spoken by the patient were, "But Doc, I had the right of way."

Did being right prevent the accident? No. Did being right eliminate pain and suffering? No. Did being right work in this case? Absolutely not.

Perhaps you don't like the theme of "Kindness" that your Character Education Committee chose for the month of October and you judge it as trite and nonspecific. You can be right about that. You can prove to yourself every day during that month how general the topic is. You can notice the non-specific nature of kindness six times a day if you choose. So what? Does being right help your students learn about kind-ness? Does it do anything to help them create a positive character? Does it get you anything other than the satisfaction of being right? Probably not.

In addition to the Basic Beliefs, six principles guide Spirit Whisperer behavior and attitudes in the classroom. In the chap-ters that follow you will learn how to apply the Principle of Suspended Judgement, the Principle of Conscious Creation, the Principle of Inner Knowing, the Principle of Personal

Responsibility, the Principle of Personal Power, and the Principle of Oneness. These six principles form the foundation of effective spirit whispering.

When you read the principles of spirit whispering listed above, did they look pretty good to you? Or did you think, "They sound self-explanatory"? If so, you may not be in sync with the first principle—the Principle of Suspended Judgement.

CHAPTER 1

The Principle of Suspended Judgement

Gregory made an important discovery the fourth week of seventh grade. He found out there are consequences associated with giving a pedestrian the finger while riding a public school bus. For four days following his spur-of-the-moment sign language choice, Gregory had to find and use a different mode of transportation to and from school.

"I've been informed by the transportation supervisor that you chose to express yourself with your middle finger yesterday," Principal Patricia Owens said as she began her discipline meeting with Gregory.

"Yeah," admitted the embarrassed middle-schooler.

"Bummer," continued Mrs. Owens. "That's sad. Community members tend to get a bit upset with that particular gesture. And of course, using your middle finger violates our school bus code of conduct. You'll need to find another way to get to school for four days.

"I like you Gregory but, like the pedestrian who saw you, I don't care for that particular behavior. In fact, when students make that choice on one of our buses, we give them a vacation from the bus for a few days. Nothing personal. It's not you, you understand. It's the behavior. The same thing happens to anyone who uses that gesture on a bus.

"I want you here at school, Gregory. I like having you here and I don't want to see you miss any of the learning that will be going on. Got any ideas on how you'll get to school for the next three weeks?"

"No."

"I sure hope you'll be able to find something. We'll miss you if you don't arrange some alternative transportation."

"Yeah."

"Would you like to hear some ideas other middle-schoolers have come up with when they chose to look for other transportation?"

"I guess so."

"Some just stay home and have their parents pick up their make-up work. Then they do their schoolwork at home while the rest of their friends are here in the classroom with the teacher. Others talk their parents into dropping them off and picking them up every day. One eighth-grader took a cab back and forth to school and paid for it out of money he'd been saving for something special. One girl rode her bike. Another got up early each morning and walked to school. She got home kind of late, though.

"I know you'll be able to handle this problem one way or the other, Gregory. I look forward to hearing how you choose to solve it. Also, here's a note to explain the situation to your parents."

"You're going to tell my parents?"

"Yes, I'm responsible for keeping parents informed of the choices children make at this school. That's part of my job description."

"Oh."

The discipline meeting described above was conducted by an educator with over twenty years of experience. This highly-skilled administrator chose to put into practice a helpful way of looking at and handling students who choose behavior that violates the school code of conduct. It's called the Principle of Suspended Judgement.

Mistakes are permitted here is one key component of the Principle of Suspended Judgement. Spirit Whisperers know that students make mistakes. Students make mistakes in subtraction, they make them while reading music, and they make them in spelling. Students also make mistakes in responsibility.

Spirit Whisperers relish students' mistakes. They lean into them and offer those mistakes back to their students as potential learning experiences. Mistakes in algebra as well as mistakes in interpersonal skills are not used for ammunition to deliver shame or criticism. Instead, they are used to extend to students an opportunity for self-discovery, correction, and learning.

A mistake holds no negative or positive value for Spirit Whisperers. Employing the Principle of Suspended Judgement, they refuse to perceive mistakes as good or bad. A mistake, in their eyes, is merely a choice that offers an opportunity for growth.

If a third-grader makes an error in subtraction and uses corrective feedback to eliminate that error for the remainder of the year, was the error good or bad? If a middle-schooler pulls the fire alarm, is confronted by the consequences of his behavior, and learns to see himself as cause rather than effect, was the alarm pulling a good thing or a bad thing? If a senior chooses to blow off studying for a government test and earns an ineligibility slip for cross-country, is that non-studying behavior on her part good or bad? Spirit Whisperers don't name the behavior "a mistake" or judge it until they witness how the student chooses to use it.

Spirit Whisperers know that there is a gift tucked away in every mistake. They react to mistakes keeping that potential treasure in mind.

Fifth-grade teacher Jerry Hutchins has worked with 11-year-old boys and girls for 10 years. He helps them learn math, U.S. history, reading, spelling, art, physical education, and English. His mathematics responsibilities include teaching long division, multiplication, division of fractions, decimals, and beginning geometry.

"You'll need your risk pads and a pencil," he informed his students recently. I watched as 31 fifth-graders located writing tools and a pile of recycled 3x5 paper slips, stapled in the upper left-hand corner. That pile of paper is what Jerry referred to as "risk pads."

"We're going to do a new kind of division today," he explained. "It's a type of division that none of you have done before. It's called long division. It's similar to the division we've already been doing, only longer. That's why you need your risk pads. I'm going to ask you to take some risks, attempt something you haven't yet done."

Jerry put a long division problem on the chalkboard and asked students to transfer it to their risk pads. I listened as he asked students to pretend they knew how to solve it. He reminded them of the value of making mistakes and how they would all learn from their own mistakes as well as from the mistakes of their classmates.

Not one fifth-grader sat motionless. Each child tackled the new challenge with effort and energy. Some had puzzled looks on their faces, but all put pencil to paper and worked on the unfamiliar problem.

After a short work period, Jerry called, "Time." He then demonstrated the correct method for working a long division problem. With the correct answer and the appropriate problem-solving method visible, Jerry chose to focus his students' attention on the importance of mistakes.

"I want to hear some really good mistakes," he said. "We can learn a lot from the mistakes we make. Who would be willing to share one of yours to help us all learn something about long division?"

Several students spoke up. Each shared a mistake and told about the thinking process that created it. Their teacher used each example as a learning opportunity and helped students see how that mistake could be avoided in the future. Mistakes were acknowledged, appreciated, and applauded.

Having worked with over 300 students during his teaching tenure, Jerry has witnessed a variety of fifth-grade attitudes toward math. Although some students appear confident and bring a positive outlook to the subject, Jerry has experienced a greater proportion of youngsters who exhibit signs of math anxiety. "They seem to choke up," he says, "and appear afraid to try anything new. It's as if they're afraid of failure. Many of my students perceive mistakes as something terrible. So they don't take risks. Obviously, that attitude hurts their math performance. That's where the idea of 'risk pads' came from."

Jerry uses risk pads in subjects other than math. Students have filled risk pads with efforts to spell "photosynthesis," define "consensus," and predict what Columbus would be doing if he were alive today. They've used them to scribble diagrams of the digestive system, create an acronym for the lessons learned about slavery, and predict what would happen when a chemical was added to a substance in a science experiment.

Regardless of the specific subject involved, the real lesson inherent in risk pads spoke to the child's spirit. This teacher used math, science, and other traditional subjects as a vehicle to teach a much larger lesson. He used the required curriculum to help students learn the value of mistakes, the beauty of taking appropriate risks, and the importance of assuming an "I can do" stance toward life.

Spirit Whisperers have learned to see students as unfinished. Perceiving students as "not yet done" is another way they put the Principle of Suspended Judgement into practice. They realize that students are on a journey, part of a process that is leading them steadily toward who they will become. They do not judge the path selected by a particular student or the stage on which she chooses to demonstrate that path. They realize that students sometimes need to get off course before they can alter their course or choose a new one.

Not only is getting "off course" not judged as good or bad by Spirit Whisperers, it isn't even seen as being off course. It is interpreted as being on course for that student—on course for receiving the perfect data to determine their next step on their individual path of becoming who they are going to be.

In fact, getting off course may be the fastest or most appropriate way for a particular child to determine a new course. Some children have to go east before they realize they want to go west. Some need to go in before they realize they like out. Some need to go up to learn the beauty inherent in down. If going up helps you appreciate down, then maybe going up wasn't off course after all. Perhaps for that student going up was the best course for learning the value of down.

Spirit Whisperers see what appears to others to be a mistake and refuse to be fooled by appearances. They realize that each student has chosen the perfect step for him or her at the present time. They remain ready to help a student make a different choice if that is what the student desires. But they remain nonjudgmental about the current choice.

The Principle of Suspended Judgement is further enhanced by a Spirit Whisperer's attitude of acceptance. Spirit Whisperers take the stance that *what is* is. They don't invest energy and effort in resisting the "what is" that shows up in their lives and in their classrooms.

If a Spirit Whisperer is assigned a class of students who are behind academically, he doesn't "should on" others. He doesn't expend energy thinking or saying:

"The middle school teachers should have . . . "

"The parents should have . . . "

"The principal should have . . . "

"Should haves" hold no value for him. Perhaps you could make a strong case that someone should have done something in a particular situation. So what? The point is no one did. *What is* is. *What is* is that these students are behind academically. Time spent "shoulding" on others and resisting *what is* is time not invested in helping those students catch up academically.

The *what is* of your classroom and of your life can be changed, but it can only be changed when you move into it, accept it for what it is, and deal with the *isness* of it. Denying *what is*, "shoulding" on others, and wishing it were different are examples of resisting the *isness*. Resistance only helps keep *what is* in place. To alter *what is*, accept it, look at it, and move into it.

If you're assigned a student who is behind in fractions or developmentally delayed, or who chooses emotional outbursts, that is *what is* for you presently. If your grade level committee selects a text that you voted against, that is the *what is* that exists for you now. If one of your student's parents persists in rescuing and bailing out their child in spite of your efforts to help that student choose responsibility, that is simply *what is*. Spirit Whisperers know that to work successfully with any of these situations they must begin by emotionally accepting *what is*.

This attitude of acceptance does not mean that you have to accept what you feel are inappropriate behaviors on the physical level. If a student cheats on tests, work to change their need to cheat. If a student rarely turns in homework assignments, continue to motivate, inspire, and implement consequences designed to encourage a different behavior. If a student is habitually tardy, use techniques and strategies to teach the student a system for being on time and a desire to use that system. Yes, work to change the behavior or attitude if you choose. But know that your efforts will more likely be successful if you begin by emotionally accepting *what is*.

Spirit Whisperers bring a certain mindset to the discipline process. They assume a stance and an attitude that can be summed up in three short sentences.

- There is no right.
- There is no wrong.
- There are consequences.

The Principle of Suspended Judgement includes operating from this mindset—that there is no right or wrong, only consequences. Mrs. Owens, the administrator who processed the discipline problem that led off this chapter, did not make Gregory wrong for using his middle finger on the bus. She did not make him bad. She did not make him awful. She did not make him terrible. She simply made him someone who needed to find alternative transportation to school for a few days.

We create a lot of problems in our schools when we make students wrong for their choices.

Think about the last time that someone made you wrong about something. Didn't you want to be right? There is a natural tendency to want to be right. We all want to be right. Our minds love to be right. All day long we run around proving how right we are about things. Our rational mind, through selective noticing, sends us constant reinforcement of how right we are.

To be right about something the mind needs a subject to be right about and someone to be in the role of being wrong. Remember the last time you felt you were right about something. I'll bet you had someone else cast in the role of being wrong. That's the way our minds work. When we make ourselves right, we simultaneously make someone else wrong. And when we make someone else wrong, they in turn want to be right.

So if you have a student who is acting out and causing trouble in your class and you make him wrong, he immediately wants to be right. That would be okay, except—for a troublemaker to be right, he has to make someone else wrong. And that someone else will most likely be you.

The only way a troublemaker knows how to make you wrong and prove to himself that he's right is to make more trouble. If your rule is "sit down," the troublemaker stands up. If your rule is "stand up," the troublemaker sits down. So eventually you get after him and make him wrong again for not following the classroom rule. The troublemaker then says to himself, "She's picking on me." "He's mean." "She's not fair." So in the troublemaker's mind, he's right and you're wrong.

By definition, when you make someone else wrong for anything, you create the other side, which then seeks to make you wrong. So if you make students wrong for their choices, you're the source of your own persecution. In fact, you're asking for it. And since you're asking for it, you're probably already getting it.

This is called the Right/Wrong Game. Spirit Whisperers steer clear of the Right/Wrong Game by refusing to play. If Jason forgets his permission slip for the field trip, don't make him wrong. Don't make him forgetful. Don't make him a procrastinator. Just make him someone who doesn't go on the field trip. If Latonia loses her library book, don't make her wrong. Don't make her bad, irresponsible, careless, or unconscious. Just make her someone who pays for the book or works it off in the library. If Jacob turns in just enough work to earn a "D", make him a person who receives a "D". Don't make him unmotivated, lazy, or wrong. Since he chose to do enough work to earn a "D", do make him a student who receives a "D".

While Spirit Whisperers don't make students wrong for their actions, they definitely hold them *accountable* for their actions. The way they hold students accountable is by implementing consequences. (See Chapter 4 for more on how Spirit Whisperers use consequences.)

Spirit Whisperers engage the Principle of Suspended Judgement and step out of the Right/Wrong Game by using a communication style that separates the deed from the doer. Many students think they are their behavior. Some think they are their report card. Others think who they are is whether or not they made the team or whether they ended up in first or fifth chair in band.

Spirit Whisperers use Teacher Talk that separates the person from their behavior.

- "I like you and I don't like that behavior."
- "That behavior is what produces a written warning here."
- "I'm sure going to miss you if you choose to drop out."
- "Nice to have you back. I'm glad you wrote a behavioral change plan during your detention that works for both of us."
- "I enjoy you and I don't appreciate that behavior."
- "Rico, I hope you'll choose a different behavior when you come back from time-out. I like seeing your smile in the group."

The notion of separating the deed from the doer is similar to what Ghandi recommended when he said, "Hate the sin, love the sinner." The sinner is not the sin. Likewise, students are not their behavior. The behavior they choose in any given moment is not who they really are. The question becomes, while not loving the act or hostile behavior, can we love and respect the child who is manifesting the behavior?

Separating the deed from the doer while you implement consequences or communicate your feelings holds the child in a state of grace for that moment. It tells her she is more than her behavior. It communicates that you see her essence—that you recognize her for who she really is, that you see beyond her present act. If we as professional educators cannot hold students in a state of grace when they choose inappropriate behaviors, who will?

Since Spirit Whisperers act as if there is no right and there is no wrong, they have no need to keep track of right and wrong. That's another way they live out the Principle of Suspended Judgement. You don't hear them say things like, "That's the fifth time this semester" or "You've interrupted me three times this period." Mental scorekeeping is an exercise that takes archeological garbage from the past and drags it into the present. Record keeping of this nature builds stress, magnifies the situation, and interferes with the process of communicating clearly and directly.

Attaching a number to the frequency of a behavior focuses the student on the pattern rather than on a specific behavior in the present moment. It encourages him to see the incident as one of a series of deficient behaviors and to create a negative picture of himself as being "that way." The past dragged into the present can easily be projected into the future, setting up a self-fulfilling prophecy.

Spirit Whisperers treat each situation as if it were new and different. They remind as if they had not reminded previously. They implement consequences as if each time was the first time they had done it. They separate the deed from the doer.

Some people have trouble with the statements "There is no right" and "There is no wrong." You may be thinking, "Some things are just right, and others are basically wrong." In one sense, right and wrong are arbitrary. They change as the situation changes and vary from one culture to another. There is nothing that is right or wrong in and of itself. A behavior or attitude is right or wrong only because we think it is, because that view fits with our personal belief system. Whatever behavior we think is right, we can find someone else who thinks it is wrong, and vice versa.

I know a school where students are expected to call teachers by their last names. They see it as a sign of respect. Another school, less than three blocks away from the first, prefers students to use teachers' first names only. That's part of how they attempt to build mutual respect between teachers and students. In each case, right and wrong are based on the collective value systems of the school personnel involved.

Even if we agree that a behavior like killing another person is wrong, would that belief change if someone was trying to kill you or your child? Doesn't right or wrong depend on the situation, the time frame, the culture or value system of the person making the judgement?

Showing up late for class is not wrong. Yes, it can be distracting to the teacher. Yes, the student could miss important information about the next test or the week's assignments. Yes, if it is more than a one-time occurrence it might call for time in the planning room. Still, it is not wrong.

Using put-downs may not help students attract or keep friends. It may not be an accurate reflection of their true essence. It might not move their cooperative group forward to task completion. It may not get them where they want to go. Still, it is not wrong.

How do you heal a troublemaker if you make him wrong for making trouble? How do you encourage the non-achiever to choose differently if you make her wrong for her present choices and interests? How will you encourage students to consider different perspectives and perceptions if you make their current perception wrong?

Making students wrong increases resistance. By not making students wrong for their actions, you create a safe place where they can look at their behaviors and learn from them. Removing right and wrong from the equation helps students focus on the behavior and the results produced.

Remember, I am *not* saying, "Anything goes." I am *not* saying, "Do whatever you want to do here in this school. It's all okay." I *am* saying that when students choose certain behaviors, there are consequences that go with those behaviors. Hold students accountable for their action. But do it without making them wrong.

Spirit Whisperers implement the Principle of Suspended Judgement by consistently seeing more in the student than the student reveals through her behaviors and attitudes. Again, Spirit Whisperers do not judge by what the student chooses to show of herself. They know there is more there. Limited beliefs, fear, and self-interference keep the student's true self under cover. As students realize that you and other significant people in their lives see them as more than the tip of the iceberg they're showing, they'll feel safe to reveal more of the fuller selves they truly are.

Seeing beyond what students reveal means seeing the fallen angel in every child. See the person who is hurting rather that the person who hurts others. Notice the child *in* pain who resides within the child who *causes* pain.

This does not mean you look the other way at inappropriate behavior. It does not mean you allow abuse and disrespect to continue. It does mean you remain at peace and operate from an open heart as you implement consequences and follow through with your discipline policy. It does mean that you take anger out of your style of discipline. It means that you activate the Principle of Suspended Judgement by looking past the appearance and recognizing the perfection that exists in every action of every moment. It means that you recognize the situation before you as being perfectly imperfect.

Spirit Whisperers steer clear of evaluation of a student, their product, effort, energy, or motivation. That is another way they manifest the Principle of Suspended Judgement.

USING PRAISE

In education, we all know and sing the value of praise. The number one behavioral modification tool in our schools today is praise. "Catch them being good" is the catch phrase of many behavior mod practitioners who believe the best way to handle inappropriate behavior is to wait until the student does something they deem as "good" and send immediate praise.

The assumptions are that praise is good, that praise builds self-esteem, that praise builds confidence. But what if that isn't always so? What if it's not always true? What if sometimes praise is not only not good but is actually destructive?

Aspirin is good, right? But is it always good? Is it always helpful? Can't aspirin be administered carelessly, capriciously, even dangerously? Sure it can, especially if it's done unconsciously. Perhaps the same can be said of praise. Let's take a closer look.

There are three distinct types of praise: *evaluative, descriptive,* and *appreciative.* The good news is that two out of the three work pretty well if our desire is to help children develop a strong internal sense of self-esteem. The problem is that the type of praise that does not build confidence and self-esteem— the type that in fact harms students by encouraging them to look away from themselves for measures of their worth, the type that creates "praise junkies" who chase external proof of their goodness—is the type we use most often. That type of praise is *evaluative* praise, and it's the kind of praise that is most common in schools, homes, and businesses today.

EVALUATIVE PRAISE

Spirit Whisperers stay conscious of the style of praise they use in their Teacher Talk repertoire and the effect it has on students. They purposefully refrain from using evaluative praise. Any praise that evaluates a student's job, product, effort, energy, motivation, or being is evaluative praise. Examples include:

- "Good job."
- "Excellent paragraph."
- "Superb design on this, Carlos."
- "That's a tremendous effort on your part."
- "Fantastic thinking!"
- "You sure are strong."
- "Very good penmanship on this paper."
- "Your project was wonderfully packaged."

Excessive evaluative praise is destructive to self-esteem, confidence, and internal motivation because it works much like a drug. It helps the child feel good for the moment. It produces a high and children get hooked on it. Once kids get hooked on the evaluative praise drug, it creates the need for more. Children begin to depend on it. They need it for measures of their own worth. Some chase after it like a junkie needing a fix. The end result is the creation of praise junkies.

I recall seeing one third-grade girl approach her art teacher, holding up her drawing and asking, "Is it good?" The art teacher, deliberately staying away from evaluative praise, filled her Teacher Talk with descriptions.

"You used five different colors," she said.

"But is it good?" the third-grader persisted.

"And you filled your entire paper," countered the art instructor.

"But is it good?" the student demanded, with no apparent way to make that decision herself.

This is clearly a child hooked on evaluative praise. To use evaluative praise as a response in this situation is to feed the dependency and continue that cycle for this student. Spirit Whisperers are not invested in creating dependent children, so they work to eliminate evaluative praise from their Teacher Talk.

Like a drug, the source of evaluative praise is external. With repeated use of this style of praise, students begin to see others as the major source of approval in their lives. It encourages them to become "externals," increasingly susceptible to external events, circumstances, and comments from others.

Another problem with evaluative praise is that it is often discounted by the recipient. Occasionally you will hear denial as out-loud talk, but most of the time students will say it to themselves and you won't hear it. The denial, or discounting, is done with self-talk and remains inside the student. Praise that is denied doesn't sink in. It has no impact. Our intent of having the child receive a positive message is thwarted.

Evaluative Praise	Denial (Self-Talk)
"You're so smart." "You've done a wonderful job." "You're really a great helper." "What a fantastic score."	"You're just saying that." "I don't think it's that good." "I'm really not like that." "It was just luck."

There are also occasions where students even have second thoughts about the person sending the evaluation and toss out the evaluator along with the evaluation.

EVALUATIVE PRAISE	DENIAL OF PRAISE AND EVALUATOR (SELF-TALK)
"That was a superb effort."	"If she thinks this is so good, she can't be very smart."
"What a great piece of art."	"That shows what he knows."

Evaluative praise is also destructive because it creates anxiety. If you can give, you can also take away. And that can be done arbitrarily or capriciously.

Some students, when they hear evaluative praise, begin looking over their shoulder, waiting for the other shoe to drop. Other students feel like they've just been put under the obligation to live up to the impossible. A common reaction to evaluative praise is for the praised child to act out or do the opposite of what was praised shortly after the original praise was delivered. It's as if they're saying, "See, I'm really not like that after all."

Evaluative praise is often an effort to manipulate the other person to get them to be more like what we want them to be. That doesn't promote self-responsibility. I recall hearing an educator at a conference I was attending present on the topic of praise.

"We need to praise each other more," he said. I agreed.

"We don't praise our students enough," he reminded us. I agreed again.

That was the last time this presenter and I were in agreement for the remainder of his presentation.

"My wife and I are grandparents," he proudly proclaimed. "We have a five-year-old granddaughter who doesn't behave very well at my son's house. We didn't want that behavior at our house so we devised a plan to manipulate her into behaving the way we want her to, using praise. We just gave her lots of positive strokes, kept telling her what a good girl she was whenever she did something right. We shaped her behavior with positive comments. We said things like, 'Good for you,' 'Good girl,' and 'That's wonderful, honey.' It took awhile, but with our positive stroke schedule, we finally got her to do what we wanted her to do." He ended the story with, "My son doesn't like it, but she minds much better at our house than she does at his."

What this speaker and many educators forget to ask themselves is, what is the goal of praise? Is the goal of praise to manipulate children into getting them to do what we want them to do? Or is it to give them clear feedback that they can use to decide for themselves who they want to be and what they want to do next? Is the goal of praise to get students to obey? Or is it to give them descriptive information they can use to develop a strong internal sense of self-esteem and worth? Is the goal of praise to get students to jump through a series of hoops deemed important by an adult in the position of authority? Or is it to help children become their own source of encouragement, provide their own motivation, and become their own bestower of reward?

Spirit Whisperers believe the goal of praise is to help students develop an internal sense of worth, to become their own source of encouragement and motivation. They use praise to increase a student's internal sense of personal power and self-esteem.

Spirit Whisperers have recognized intuitively that there are two parts to every praise exchange. They also know which one of those parts is the most important. Those two parts of praise are: (1) my words; (2) the student's words.

Every time I praise another, either orally or in writing, I get to choose which words to use. That begins the two-step praise process. If my words are evaluative, they look or sound like this:

- "You did a good job."
- "That's excellent."
- "You're awesome."

The second part of every praise exchange is the student's words. Since it's usually done as self-talk, we don't often hear those words. It's the second part—what the person says to him- or herself about the praise—that has the greatest effect on self-esteem, self-responsibility, internal motivation, and the child's spirit. If I say, "Tremendous effort," and the student's self-talk is, "It only took me 10 minutes," whose words have the most effect? If I say, "Really good project," and Robert says to himself, "Carlos's was better," whose words have the most influence?

Spirit Whisperers understand that it's not what someone else says to you that's important, but rather what you say to yourself about what they say to you. That is where your power lies. That is where you are clearly in control. They apply that concept when they consciously structure and send praise.

A Spirit Whisperer's goal is to structure her Teacher Talk to leave room for the student to make the evaluation. She wants the *child's* words to be "good," "excellent," "tremendous." A Spirit Whisperer wants the child *to say to himself*, "I did a great job." "This is a fantastic project." "I've got good handwriting."

If *our* words evaluate, we're trying to take self-esteem from the outside and place it on the inside of the student. If the *student's* words evaluate, then the self-esteem comes from the inside and is drawn out. The student's self-esteem becomes internal rather than external.

The way a Spirit Whisperer leaves room for the student to make the evaluation is by choosing words that are descriptive and/or appreciative.

DESCRIPTIVE PRAISE

Descriptive praise describes. It *affirms* what has been done rather that *evaluates* what has been done. It speaks to accomplishments. Examples are:

- "You indented every paragraph."
- "Your margins fell within the 3/4 inch guidelines and all your words were legible."
- "You got 16 out of 18 and showed all your work."
- "Every picture on your paper begins with B."
- "Everyone in here began working in the first two minutes."
- "That's 2 feet, 7 inches farther than you've thrown it before."
- "Your project met all the criteria and exceeded the creativity guidelines by 10 points."

When teachers praise descriptively, they allow the student to draw his own conclusions. The evaluation becomes internal, and the evaluation is delivered by a person the student is more likely to believe: himself. When the praise is believed, self-esteem grows.

APPRECIATIVE PRAISE

Appreciative praise expresses appreciation. It usually includes the words "I appreciate" or "thank you" somewhere in the communication. This alternative to evaluative praise tells the student what behaviors are helpful and specifies any positive effects a behavior has on your life or on that of the other students. Examples include:

- "I appreciate your cooperation with the substitute teacher yesterday. It makes me look like I'm doing my job. Thanks."
- "Thank you for running the video camera. I'll use the tape to improve my teaching."
- "I was so happy to see the sink cleaned and realize I didn't have to clean it before I went home. I appreciate your efforts."
- "Class, thank you all for getting your business letter in on time. That saves me from having to go back and add latecomers into my grade book."

With appreciative praise the teacher makes a statement that once again allows the student to draw her own conclusion. If your Teacher Talk is, "Thank you for passing back the papers. That saved me five minutes," the student concludes, "I really helped out." If your words to a parent are, "Thank you for coming on the trip. It reduces my stress when other adults are along to help out," the parent concludes, "I am valuable." In each case, the teacher's words leave room for the person receiving the praise to make the evaluation.

Descriptive and appreciative praise are often linked together in the same verbalization.

- "That's the fifth box of books you carried out to my car. [Descriptive] You're saving my sore back. Thanks." [Appreciative]

- "The questions you asked the guest speaker were topic-related and showed you were listening. [Descriptive] I could see the smile on her face and hear the energy in her voice as she answered them." [Appreciative]

Both descriptive and appreciative praise allow the student to draw the conclusion and to make the evaluation. With each, self-worth becomes internal. The student becomes the source of his own approval. He becomes the measure of his own success. When praise comes from the inside out, rather than from the outside in, it's harder to discount.

When tempted to use evaluative praise, stop. Make your Teacher Talk appreciative and descriptive, leaving the evaluation to the student.

A final point about appreciative, descriptive, and evaluative praise is that the teacher's job is to teach. There is *no* teaching in evaluative praise. There is only evaluation. If you write simply, "Good job," across the top of a student's composition, how do they know what was good? How do they know what to reproduce next time?

Descriptive praise teaches. It spells out specifically what part of the assignment or behavior met the criteria and why. Appreciative praise also teaches. It informs the student how the assignment or behavior affected others.

While Spirit Whisperers work very hard to keep evaluation out of their teaching, they recognize that evaluation is part of their jobs. In fact, if they don't evaluate students they run the risk of being fired. Many Spirit Whisperers are often required to use grading systems that evaluate student progress based on criteria over which they and their students have little control.

As often as possible, Spirit Whisperers set up their grading procedures descriptively. Students know ahead of time what criteria need to be met for an "A", what they need to do to earn a "B", etc. They work to eliminate subjectivity and judgement from their grading system and to remove surprises.

USING FEEDFORWARD

In addition to keeping evaluation out of their praise, Spirit Whisperers also keep it out of their directive feedback. Every student needs directive feedback from time to time, or, as it's referred to in the Performance Learning Systems[*] materials, *feedforward*. I like the term "feedforward" because it reminds me that what I want to offer students is direction, not correction. Feedforward, as used by Performance Learning Systems, is designed to give students an opportunity to move forward by telling them what needs to be corrected or by giving them information on why they were successful.

When a student's work or behavior does not meet criteria or approach the standard, directive feedforward is helpful. If we don't send feedforward in these instances, we communicate to the student that any old effort or result will do. By not sending directive feedforward, we send students messages like:

- "I didn't notice."
- "I don't care."
- "It doesn't matter."
- "You don't matter."

Spirit Whisperers don't send those messages to students. They realize that sending healthy, non-evaluative, directive feedforward messages is necessary from time to time, and when they send them they keep in mind the following guidelines.

---

[*] Performance Learning Systems offers graduate courses that teach educators techniques and strategies consistent with the Spirit Whisperer concepts. For information about relevant courses, see the appendix.

1. Make feedforward specific.

Praise and feedforward are closely related. They are flip sides of the same coin. Feedforward, like praise, can be delivered in evaluative, descriptive, or unappreciative terms.

Evaluative feedforward resembles and feels like criticism. "Terrible," "ugly," "sloppy," "poor," "disgusting," and "awful" are too general to be useful and are examples of feedforward turned critical. Evaluative criticism ("Your cleanup job was terrible," or "That's a poor effort"), like evaluative praise, gives the student little information that can be used effectively and turned into improvement.

It is not helpful for the student to hear the cleanup job was terrible unless he knows specifically *why* you think so. It's of little benefit for the youngster to know her effort was poor unless she knows exactly *what* was poor. Without specifics, a child can make no corrective change. Correction cannot happen without direction.

2. Feedforward describes what needs to be done and/or tells what you don't appreciate.

If you tell a first-grader his desk has paste on it and that wet cloths usually do the trick on sticky desks, you give him specific information he can use to improve his cleanup effort.

If you tell your middle-schooler that her paragraph contains three different topics, you give the kind of information that can be used to improve her writing.

When you are descriptive with your feedforward, giving specific information about what you like and why, the student is provided valuable information from which to learn. However, if your remarks are evaluative, the student is left wondering what wasn't good enough.

Sharing displeasure or giving information about what you would appreciate in the future is another way of giving your students useful feedforward. For example:

- "I'm sure Mrs. Jacobson, the custodian, won't appreciate all the scraps I see on the floor. It'll take her a lot longer to do her job tonight unless we all help out."

- "I would appreciate it if you would put your history notebook in order according to the table of contents on the board. That makes it much easier for me to locate what I need to find."

Students generally respond better when you share what you would appreciate or describe what you don't like than they do if you criticize with evaluation. You'll get a more positive response by stating, "Paint brushes need to be rinsed out and left in the large can on the shelf. Spills need to be wiped up with a sponge or they get tracked around the room," than you will by saying, "This paint area is a sloppy mess." You will encourage greater cooperation and model more respect when your remark is, "I don't enjoy being interrupted. I lose my focus," than when you say, "You're rude and inconsiderate."

3. THE MAIN FUNCTION OF FEEDFORWARD IS TO POINT OUT WHAT NEEDS TO BE ACCOMPLISHED IN A SITUATION.

- "Please show all your work on the last three problems."
- "Added detail to this section would help me understand your conclusion."
- "I need you to wait until I'm finished speaking before you begin."

- "To look like a group, all members need to be pulled in tight, leaning forward, and looking at one another."

Feedforward gives direction. It communicates what needs to be done. It points the way.

4. Feedforward does not attack character or personality.

Students often hear feedback that evaluates as an attack. They believe it is aimed directly at them, and they take it personally. Resentment, resistance, and defensiveness follow. If you learn to use Teacher Talk that speaks to the situation instead of the person and mentions *what* was done rather than *who* did it, there is less chance that students will take offense. Spirit Whisperers choose words that focus on what was or what was not accomplished, what is included or is missing from their expectation, what they specifically like or dislike.

"I see a library book on the floor. Books belong on or in desks" focuses on the book and specifically describes the situation. "You're so irresponsible" draws attention to the person and does not offer instruction or useful information. "You people are too noisy" puts the spotlight on the students. "The noise has exceeded our agreed upon level" points to the problem.

Spirit Whisperers use a variety of techniques to actualize the Principle of Suspended Judgement. Seeing students as unfinished, appreciating mistakes, carrying an attitude of acceptance, holding students accountable without making them right or wrong, separating the deed from the doer, seeing more in the student than she sees in herself, using descriptive and appreciative praise along with evaluation-free feedforward are valuable instruments in the Spirit Whisperer's toolbox. They are tools a Spirit Whisperer uses with students, but the

Spirit Whisperer also uses them with him- or herself to keep free of the judgement trap.

Judgement is a trap. It limits vision and narrows perspective by keeping us prisoners of our own interpretations. Judgement labels and categorizes. It places people in categories and leaves little room for exception.

Judgements make permanent. They tend to be self-fulfilling and final. If you judge a student as unmotivated and use language and behavior that communicates that belief to her, you increase the chance she will act in ways that match your belief. Since you are more likely to notice evidence of unmotivated behavior in this student, your selective noticing system creates that perception as reality for you. The student then has to become extra-motivated before you release her from the trap of your judgement.

Not only are judgements a trap, they're often inaccurate. Spirit Whisperers know they don't have enough information to make accurate judgements.

If I told you a man on the bus failed to give his seat to a pregnant woman carrying packages, you may judge him as inconsiderate. If I explained further that he wore dark glasses and carried a white cane, you might make a different judgement. If you learned later that he was only impersonating a blind man, you'd have still another judgement.

A final tool used by Spirit Whisperers to suspend judgement is the tool of knowing that they don't know. What we don't know is always more that what we do know in any situation. That includes what we know about education, what we know about ourselves, and what we know about our students.

Knowing that you don't know does not diminish what you do know in any way, but it does help you to put what you do know in perspective and allows you to keep an open mind toward what others know. When you know that you don't know, then what you do know can become part of a mutual dialogue and lead to more of what we know collectively.

When you judge a student, you judge her on the basis of insufficient information. You don't know what it's like to live in that person's skin. You cannot see the world through her eyes.

Judgement tells more about the one who is judging than it does about the person being judged. Judging does not happen because of what you observe in your world. It happens because the observer within you chooses to judge. When you judge another, your judgement says very little about the person being judged. But it screams loudly to the world that you are a person who needs to judge.

When you teach to a child's spirit, when you send a lesson in love, cooperation, or caring, if you do so with judgement attached, you undermine the teaching. Students have built-in integrity detectors. When judgement accompanies the teaching, the teaching is ignored. Remove judgement from your teaching. Let it lie dormant on the shelf as you activate the Principle of Suspended Judgement.

Practice the Principle of Suspended Judgement as you read through the remainder of this book. Play with the notion that what you don't know is more than what you do know about the students you have attracted into your life. Then see if you can fit it with the theme of the next chapter, "The Principle of Inner Knowing."

CHAPTER 2

The Principle of Inner Knowing

"I'm not sure if I should do my report on Balboa or Magellan," a sixth-grader explained to her social studies teacher.

A high school counselor heard, "I like choir, but I'm also interested in that new environmental studies class."

"Should I give my art work to my mother or to my father?" asked a puzzled second-grader.

Although these comments were made by students of different ages, and uttered in different parts of the country, the response by each attending adult was the same: "Check it out inside."

"Check it out inside" is a Teacher Talk response often used by Spirit Whisperers to help students look within for answers. Each of us has a wise part within, an intuitive part that knows what is best for us. Learning how to contact, listen to, and trust that inner authority are important skills. They are invaluable when life presents us with problems whose answers are not found in the back of the book.

Part of our job as teachers, counselors, coaches, or administrators—or as any adult whose responsibilities include working with young people—is helping students learn where to turn for answers. Typically, we show them how to look up words in the dictionary, consult experts, use an encyclopedia, access the Internet, and read the newspaper. Or we equip them with the skills they need to use a reference librarian effectively. In dealing with questions or matters of a factual nature, this is an appropriate and necessary part of a student's education. But as readily and effectively as we teach our students how to use a variety of external sources for answers, rarely do we turn them around and teach them to look inward for answers that can only be found within.

Spirit Whisperers believe that when we teach students to look away from themselves for the most important answers in life, we have them facing in the wrong direction. Spirit Whisperers honor the Principle of Inner Knowing and help students look inward by using the phrase and philosophy, "Check it out inside."

All of us know what we need to know. It's in every one of us. Call it gut-level feeling, intuition, inner knowing, conscience, listening to God, the wise part within, inner authority, or whatever other label you're comfortable using. Regardless of its name, it is there, waiting to be accessed whenever we are ready and able to call it forth.

Certainly, it's important to teach students to check their inner knowing against other forms of knowing. Encourage them to test their gut-level feeling by checking it against what they discover from other sources. Invite them to consult other experts or ask a friend. Have them read up on their area of concern. And when all the data are present, encourage students to allow their inner wisdom to be the final authority.

"I don't want my kid doing any of that inner listening," a father announced dramatically in the middle of one of my parenting seminars recently. "I teach my kid to listen to me. That's what I train him to do, and that's what he better do."

After he finished, I began my explanation. "That works okay when children are young, especially when health and safety issues are a concern. The problem occurs later, when children grow into the preteen and teen years. By that time, if your child has learned to respond only to an outside authority . . ."

As soon as the words "outside authority" entered his consciousness, this agitated dad interrupted again. "*Outside authority*. Those words sound good to me. That's what I want my kid to do, respond to an outside authority. And *I'm* the outside authority my kid better be responding to."

After he sat back down, I finished my response to his expressed concern. I'm not sure he heard or understood my point of view that night, but I think the other parents in the audience did. I explained that the biggest problem with training kids to listen to an outside voice occurs in adolescence. At that time in a child's life, the outside voice changes from the parent to the peer group.

If a child has not learned to listen to and hear her inside voice by adolescence, she is highly susceptible to pressure from peers. It requires a strong internal sense of self to stand in your peer group at age 13 and say to yourself, "This doesn't feel right. This doesn't resonate for me with my values. I think I better hold off on this right now and back up a couple of steps." This is a tough stance for any child to take—doubly tough for a kid with little practice listening inwardly.

Even with the best of intentions, trying to follow what you have been told is more difficult than following what you, yourself, know. Self-generated wisdom is not as easily dismissed as wisdom that comes from an outside authority. Having faith in his own inner authority serves a student well by enabling him to resist the temptation to please others at his own expense or to compromise himself by conforming to peer pressure.

Trusting inner authority is not like a light bulb you can flip on when your child turns 14. It needs to brighten slowly over time and grow stronger with continued use. If the inner voice of spirit is discouraged or ignored in young people and goes unused, their instincts can lie dormant, depriving them of an important source of knowledge.

Spirit Whisperers do not seek to be the authority in students' lives. They strive, instead, to help each child develop her own inner authority and learn to hear the voice of spirit within herself. Spirit Whisperers engage the Principle of Inner Knowing by helping their students develop an internal standard. When you know from a place of inner authority—and you know that you know—then you can trust your own judgement regarding drugs, sex, alcohol, and other important issues. With that increased confidence, you are not as likely to rely solely on the judgement of your peer group.

Students who have had opportunities to check it out inside develop their inner authority to the point where they become their own rule maker. They develop internal standards and decide when they are doing well and when they aren't. They know where they are in relationship to those standards. It is *their* determination of how well they're doing that becomes their primary form of assessment.

A high school band director recently told me of his efforts to help his students develop an internal standard. They had just returned from a weekend competition where they had played four songs. The band was given two "1's" and two "2's" by the judge who evaluated the performances. Since "1" is the highest score awarded, the band did pretty well compared to the competitive standard against which they were being judged.

On Monday, the first day of school following the competition, this instructor put his students in sections (horns, drums, woodwinds, etc.) and had them discuss several questions he had designed to help them debrief their recent experience. He challenged his students to rate themselves as a band and discuss how they thought they had done based on what they knew about their capabilities and their performance.

The consensus of these students was that they agreed with one of the "1's" they received. The other "1" they thought should have been a "2". They agreed that they had played that selection better right there in the band room the week preceding the competition. They knew on the inside that they had not given their best performance on that piece the day of the competition. They also agreed with one of the "2's" they were awarded. The other "2" they had received they questioned. Students felt it should have been a "1". "We nailed that piece," one student told the band instructor. The others agreed.

The most interesting part of this story is what the instructor told me next. "You know," he mused, "they were right on. In fact, I think my students' interpretation of their efforts and performance was more accurate than that of the judge. I felt their evaluation rang true for how they played that day."

These high-schoolers didn't need a judge present at their music competition. They needed no outside authority to rate and evaluate them. They were capable of handling that responsibility themselves. They were able to judge their own performance and do it accurately because they had developed an internal standard. They knew what a quality performance sounded like, and they could tell when they had achieved it and when they hadn't. They needed no outside evaluator telling them what score they earned. They knew it the moment they were done playing. They could feel it on the inside.

These students didn't acquire that degree of inner knowing by accident. They developed it over time, with the help of a
Spirit Whisperer who guided them through numerous opportunities to self-assess and debrief their performances. Their
inner knowing grew the same way students improved the play
of their individual instruments: slowly, with regular practice—
resulting in steady improvement.

Other students around the country are learning about an
internal standard by playing the game of Mummy Ball. With
Mummy Ball, students sit on desks or stand and throw a soft,
spongy Nerf ball around the room. The game derives its name
from the fact that you have to be mum when you play it. If you
talk, you have eliminated yourself.

The game of Mummy Ball has few rules. Those that do
exist include the nonverbal aspect of the activity and a simple
procedure. First, the game does not begin until the room is
cleaned and everyone is ready to leave for the day. Then students play what appears at first glance to be a simple game of
catch. The ball is thrown around the room and students are
eliminated if they throw a ball that can't be caught or drop a
throw they could have caught.

But Mummy Ball as taught and implemented by Spirit
Whisperers is much more than a game of catch. It's a game of
moral judgement and an effort to build an internal authority
within students. There is no umpire, no linesperson, no referee
in Mummy Ball. Students find no officials to look to for enforce-
ment of the rules or for decisions on close plays.

Our traditional games of baseball, football, basketball,
hockey and soccer have a built-in, forced reliance on officials.
Each of our most popular games has an external, arbitrary
judge—someone who decides things. And children learn, over
time, to look away from themselves and toward others for those

judgements. That breeds dependence on others and diminishes self-responsibility and self-trust.

In Mummy Ball, students make the decisions. The thrower sits down if he determines that his throw was uncatchable. The receiver eliminates herself if she feels the throw was in reach and she could have caught it. Each person makes an individual decision based on their own picture of their unique abilities.

It is possible that after a throw was not caught the thrower and receiver both sit down. The thrower determines for herself that the throw could have been more accurate. The receiver figures he could have caught the same throw. So both sit down.

It is also possible that neither person eliminates himself or herself following a missed throw. The thrower decides that the throw was accurate enough and continues in the game. The receiver decides that the throw was too difficult to catch, so remains a participant. Each person makes their own decision independent of the other, based on their own interpretation of their own ability.

There is no appeal to an external authority, no argument before high tribunals. Each student's decision is final. The notion that each student is the best judge of his or her own capabilities is respected. Students making value judgements on another student's decision must keep those judgements to themselves. If they speak up, they are eliminated because they have violated the Mummy Ball rule of silence.

Obviously, some players are better at practicing moral judgement than others are. Students have found a way on their own to equalize the situation. Mummy Ball participants who make consistent and blatant errors in judgement find that they don't receive the ball as often as they had in the past. They get the message and change their judgements and behavior.

Teachers report that their biggest challenge with Mummy Ball is staying free of the enforcer role. Students typically look to the teacher when one of them makes what appears to be a poor judgement. They want the teacher to fix it. They expect the teacher to make everyone play fair. Many students find it more comfortable to continue their practice of looking away from themselves to others to make the important decisions of fair/unfair, right/wrong, in/out.

Watch Mummy Ball from your desk without becoming involved in the game or succumbing to the subtle invitations to become a referee. Find something else to do while you keep one eye on the action. Monitor your own internal reaction to the game and the way it's being played. Check out where you are on the issue of trusting that students know what they know and that inner knowing must be developed with practice, over time. Check out your urge to rescue and fix things. Play with letting it be okay that the game is unfolding in a way that is perfectly imperfect. Allow Mummy Ball to be a learning experience for everyone, including yourself.

You won't find the benefits of Mummy Ball reflected in state assessment test scores. There is no column for it in a student's permanent record. It's not even listed on a report card. It certainly doesn't show up as a performance objective on any grade-level list.

Yet, Spirit Whisperers know what they know. And they know that in our competitive culture, with its emphasis on winning and losing, on the compiling of statistics that rank and separate, and on forced reliance on an outside authority, Mummy Ball's simplicity and focus on personal decision-making is refreshing. It challenges students to look within and to respond with integrity and self-responsibility. Spirit Whisperers need no more tangible proof of Mummy Ball's effectiveness than their own inner knowing. They simply know it is worth the time invested—so they do it.

How well do your students make moral judgements? How developed are their internal standards? What is their inner knowing quotient? Why not check it out with Mummy Ball?

Another way Spirit Whisperers implement the Principle of Inner Knowing and help students develop an inner standard is through the use of self-evaluation activities. Typically, teachers own and wield the red pencil. Teachers mark on students' papers. Teachers decide what work needs to be done over. It is teachers who determine what is quality work and what isn't in most classrooms. Is it any wonder that our current educational system produces students weak in self-assessment skills?

Involving students in evaluation activities is as simple as passing out a file card and having each student rate the movie they just viewed. Share with them your objectives in showing the movie, and ask how close this movie came to achieving those objectives for them personally. Give the criteria on which you want the movie judged; i.e., content, interest, humor, relevance to the topic. Ask students to give each category a "1" to "5" rating. Have them explain their rating with a two-sentence explanation.

In addition to giving students some practice with evaluation procedures, you will have involved them in the running of your classroom by seeking their input. This builds a sense of belonging and helps the students feel useful. Also, you will have given them an opportunity to think critically while bringing what they know and observed to the task at hand. While this process unfolds, students are actually using the information from the content of the movie for a specific, useful purpose. Using the information increases retention.

A first-grade teacher I observed recently had her students working on a penmanship lesson. Each student was printing a full page of M's, taking care to get the letters right between the lines. When the students finished, this teacher announced, "Boys and girls, please look over your page of M's. Circle the two you think are your best. I'll be looking over your papers tonight and I want to know which ones *you* think are your best. Now put a box around two that are not your best M's. These would be the two that you might do over if we were going to do them over. We aren't going to do them over now. Just put a box around those two so I call tell which ones they are."

With a 90-second self-evaluation exercise, the Spirit Whisperer in charge communicated a lot to her students. Without saying so directly, she showed them they had the power of discernment. She communicated that she did not see herself as totally responsible for judging their work. She told them by her actions that they, too, were responsible for determining quality. She was helping them create a standard of quality that was true for them, a standard that they would carry around with them wherever they went.

The teacher who designed this self-evaluation lesson took the penmanship papers home to add descriptive and appreciative praise as well as feedforward comments as needed. It's important to note that this Spirit Whisperer did not confine her comments to her students' penmanship only. She also commented on their efforts to self-evaluate. "I agree," "You were certainly able to tell which ones are your best," and "I see what you mean," she wrote on their papers, helping them see that their experience with self-evaluation was noticed and appreciated. In her mind, self-evaluation was as important as penmanship in this particular lesson.

After several days with similar opportunities to self-evaluate using R's, L's, P's, and S's, imagine these students working on a page of T's. Now, with a growing internal standard of excellence, a child who creates a T that is not up to standard knows it. Knowing the T that he just made is not one of his best, he is more likely to stop, erase it, and create one that more closely fits his personal standard of excellence.

Without these opportunities to self-evaluate, the same child isn't as likely to recognize the poor quality of his latest T. In addition, having a less developed internal standard of personal best, he doesn't even see judging the quality of letters as his job. In his mind, that job belongs to his teacher.

Another early childhood educator asks students on occasion to put a P on the top of their paper if they are proud of it. Other times she has them add an N for neat or an H if they are happy with their product or effort. Over time, she intends to help wean these youngsters from their reliance on external measures of success: the stars, stickers, and smiley faces that are awarded indiscriminately in many classrooms today, teaching children that others know better than they do about the quality of their own work.

A sixth-grade teacher passes out copies of report cards to his students prior to parent/teacher conferences. He asks them to grade themselves and fill out the entire card as if they were the one doing the reporting. "If you think you're doing well in math and I don't, we need to talk about it," he advises them. "Also, if I think you're doing well and you don't, we need to talk about that, too." He fills out the official report card based on the assessment data he has accumulated during the marking period. Prior to conferences with the parents, this teacher has a conference with each child, comparing the report he produced to the one they created for themselves.

The band instructor, teachers who invest time in Mummy Ball, the early childhood educator who had students circle their two best letters, and the sixth-grade teacher who had students fill out their own report cards have something in common. They each believe that inner knowing and development of an internal standard improve and grow with practice. And they each believe it is their job as professional educators to provide those practice opportunities for students.

Another way in which Spirit Whisperers help students touch that wise part within is through the act of debriefing. Spirit Whisperers debrief often and with purpose. Again, their goal is to teach to the child's spirit so that the student can increasingly tap into that important resource.

Debriefing can be defined as an opportunity to help students look at their behaviors and the impact of those behaviors so they can learn from them.

We've all heard the axiom "You learn by doing." "You learn from your experience" is a similar catch phrase. Many educators subscribe to these notions, and their belief in them has led to the increase of manipulative materials and "hands on" activities in classrooms throughout the country. Many teachers think that getting students actively involved in learning speeds learning and increases retention. The idea is that you can learn more about using a computer if you have a computer to use. Learning to ride a horse is easier if horses are available to ride. Learning to dance happens more quickly if you get up and move your feet than it does if you sit in your chair and read about it.

While Spirit Whisperers see the truth in the we-learn-from-experience philosophy, they also believe the opposite—that we *don't* learn from our experience. Spirit Whisperers are able to hold that dichotomy in their minds and make sense out of both views. They make neither statement wrong, and see the truth and benefits in each.

John Dewey once said, "You don't learn from your experience. You learn from processing your experience." John Dewey was talking about debriefing. If we all learned from our experience, no one would have to get drunk twice. Once would be enough. If we all learned from our experience, all second marriages would work. Or as one workshop participant suggested, "If we all learned from our experience, there would be no second marriages."

Spirit Whisperers agree with Dewey. We don't learn from our experience, we learn from debriefing it. Certainly much was learned from the tragic Columbine High School experience. But more learning resulted from the debriefings that followed it. Students debriefed. Faculty debriefed. So did the local police, the FBI, hospital staff, SWAT team members, parents, administrators, and ambulance drivers. Because of the exhaustive debriefing which followed this horrific event, notebooks full of what was learned were collected, preserved, and shared with others.

While debriefing of the Columbine High School experience took months, Spirit Whisperers have learned to shorten that time frame to minutes and still retain the benefits derived from processing students' experiences. They debrief regularly in time frames that usually fall under 15 minutes in length.

Debriefing begins with an experience. If two of your students fight on the playground, congratulations—you've just had an experience. If you get a note from the substitute teacher suggesting that you never invite her back because of the rudeness of your class, you've just had an experience. If that note describes instead the self-responsible behaviors exhibited by your students and the substitute asks to be invited back in the future, that too is an experience. A field trip, a messy lunchroom, a guest speaker, abuse of the microscopes, and group work all qualify as an experience.

After students have an experience, the teacher helps them to reflect on it by thinking about it, talking about it, and writing about it. Two or three questions or statements are selected by the teacher to focus students' thinking. Students react to those statements/questions orally, in writing, or both.

Following an experience of two days with a substitute teacher, a regular classroom teacher announced, "Apparently some of you chose some interesting behaviors when the sub was here last week. I'd like to get your perspective on what happened so I can understand it from your point of view. I have three statements I'm going to put on the overhead. Please react privately and nonverbally to each statement in writing. We'll do a share-and-compare with your responses shortly."

The following statements were displayed:

1. MY LEVEL OF RESPECT WHEN THE SUBSTITUTE TEACHER WAS HERE:

0 1	2 3	4 5 6	7 8 9	10
LOW		MODERATE		HIGH

    WRITE A TWO-SENTENCE RATIONALE TO EXPLAIN YOUR ANSWER.
2. ONE THING I NOTICED THAT WAS RESPECTFUL WAS _____.
3. ONE THING I COULD DO NEXT TIME TO INCREASE MY LEVEL OF RESPECT WOULD BE _____.

After four minutes of writing time, the teacher invited students to share their reactions with a partner. She then led a total group discussion during which several students volunteered their written reactions. The teacher refrained from judging or commenting on the shared reactions. She opted instead to listen to the ideas being presented and paraphrase them, thus demonstrating her understanding of those ideas.

At the conclusion of the class discussion, this teacher asked students to build a class list describing what they had learned about respect from reflecting on this experience with the substitute teacher. This is the list that was generated.

1. WE WEREN'T AS RESPECTFUL AS WE COULD HAVE BEEN.
2. WE DID DO RESPECTFUL THINGS.
3. IT'S HARD TO SHOW RESPECT IF YOU'RE NOT GETTING ANY.
4. SOME OF US DID BETTER THAN OTHERS.
5. IT'S NOT ALWAYS EASY TO CHOOSE RESPECT.

A typical response to an agitated note from a substitute teacher in our current educational climate would be a stern lecture from the regular classroom teacher. Sharing of alleged transgressions, disappointment, and threats would be the order of the day. The lecture would be an attempt on the part of a well-intentioned educator to fill a perceived void from the outside in. Intentions aside, that approach would violate the Principle of Inner Knowing.

Spirit Whisperers replace lecturing with debriefing. Debriefing, a skill taught thoroughly in Performance Learning Systems graduate credit courses, is an attempt to pull out what already exists within students. It calls forth their inner knowing, helping them stay conscious of what they know so they can examine their behavior in light of that knowledge. Debriefing approaches the issues of respect and responsibility by drawing from the inside out rather than by attempting to work from the outside in.

Employing the Principle of Inner Knowing, a Spirit Whisperer would welcome a conflict concerning the execution of Mummy Ball. She would realize that Mummy Ball was merely the water being splashed around in on that particular day. The lesson would be about spirit and creation of an inner standard of integrity, regardless of the temperature or depth of the water (content). Ignoring the urge to lecture about right/wrong and fair/unfair, she would reach into her toolkit and design debriefing questions that encouraged learning to surface.

"Class," one teacher told her seventh-graders, "it's come to my attention that some of you are frustrated with playing Mummy Ball. I've had complaints that some of you are perceived as not eliminating yourselves when it might be appropriate to do so. I want to share some of my observations of Mummy Ball with you and solicit your reactions to them.

"I have seen, on occasion, a throw that sailed over the receiver's head by two feet and neither person sat down. I've seen this happen more than once. I have also observed incidents of a throw hitting the receiver in their hands and, again, neither person sat down. I believe these types of incidents are on the increase. At least I'm beginning to notice them more often.

"As you know, in Mummy Ball, it is each person's responsibility to decide for themselves whether or not they could have caught the ball or thrown it more accurately. You decide about your own abilities and skill level. You decide about fairness. You each decide the degree of integrity you bring to the game. It would be my guess that some of you are choosing to take that responsibility more seriously than others are. Let's find out what you think about this situation and discuss what we can do to make the game more fun for everyone."

This teacher then displayed three debriefing questions that asked students to reflect on their experience of Mummy Ball and invited them to write their reactions.

1. WITH REGARD TO FAIRNESS AND MUMMY BALL, OUR CLASS IS
   - very fair
   - somewhat fair
   - not very fair
   WRITE A ONE-SENTENCE RESPONSE TO EXPLAIN YOUR ANSWER.

2.   WE COULD MAKE MUMMY BALL MORE FAIR IF EACH
     PERSON WOULD _____.
3.   SOMETHING I WANT TO REMEMBER DURING MUMMY
     BALL IS _____.

The instructor then organized students into groups of five and had them compare and discuss answers to the first debriefing question. A total class discussion of that question followed. Perceptions varied. The final two statements were verbalized by going up and down rows, giving students the opportunity to share or pass. Everyone who wanted to contribute was heard. No conclusions were drawn, no lessons listed. Experiencing the process was enough.

Did this debriefing activity alter the execution of Mummy Ball in this classroom? Of course it did. By putting the issue on the table and raising students' consciousness of the effect their behavior was having, and by hearing each other's frustrations and concerns, students moved to a new awareness and a new level of responsibility in their approach to the game.

Debriefing questions/statements call for self-assessment. Students are asked to rate themselves, the class, or their work group on such issues as following directions, cleanup, respect for the microscopes, getting started quickly, ignoring distractions, disagreeing politely, taking turns, and sharing materials. Many experiences occur throughout the year where students can be given opportunities to practice self-appraisal. As with subtraction, speaking a second language, and using a keyboard, the more students practice, the better they become.

Debriefing questions/statements ask for higher-level thinking. Some questions demand analysis. (What grade would you give our class on its effort to get started quickly today?) Others require inductive thinking. (What generalizations can you make about the way we respond to distractions?) Some ask students to engage in the process of prediction. (What do you expect will happen if we put this cleanup plan into operation tomorrow?) Additional debriefing questions ask students to compare and contrast, prioritize, describe patterns, set goals, summarize, and come up with options. All invite thinking.

Since debriefing statements ask for student opinion, all answers are right answers. Students are invited to look inside and access their own ideas, feelings, and beliefs. They listen to the thoughts of others and draw their own conclusions. The Principle of Inner Knowing means that no one else has your answer. It also means that you have no one else's answer.

Students benefit from hearing the shared reactions of others even if they choose to participate minimally in the written portion of the debriefing. Spirit Whisperers choose not to push for specific conclusions or learnings from students since they recognize that readiness is something that can't be forced. They know they don't have to score all their runs in the first inning. There are many innings in each game and an abundance of games during the year. Since they realize they will come up to bat (debrief) often, they relax and trust the process.

Debriefing is one more attempt on the part of Spirit Whisperers to help students develop inner authority. No outside authority, no set of rules, no laws can provide the specific guidance that is needed in day-to-day living. Students must learn to hear their own voice of truth and create their own ethic in order to live in alignment with spirit in today's world.

Watch the behavior of shoppers in the express lane at a large grocery store. Count the number of items that customers place on the checkout stand at the 10-and-under lane. It won't take long before you notice people with 12, 15, and even 20 items going through that lane. What's going on here? These people can count. These people can read. Can't they?

Shoppers with 17 items in a 10-and-under lane on a busy day are short on inner guidance. They rely on outside authority to keep them within the norms of society and have learned to numb out to conscience.

Other people become slaves to rules and behave obediently no matter what the circumstance. If you hang around a grocery store long enough you will eventually observe the shopper with 11 items who lines up behind four customers with full grocery baskets even though the 10-and-under lane is empty. Blindly obedient, this person follows the store guidelines without thinking through the ethics involved. He has not learned to touch that wise part within that sends us information about adjusting guidelines and becoming our own rule maker. He is not thinking for himself.

Helping students listen to and trust their inner knowing is made doubly difficult because many people in authority teach students to distrust that wise part within. "Stop listening to yourself" is the message that is sent. "Listen to me. Listen to us. Follow our rules. We know best. We know what is right. We have the way." Those are the implied, if not spoken, messages consistently directed to young people in many schools, churches, and youth organizations. Leaders in these organizations have forgotten that the voice within can be a greater reminder than can any outside influence.

Shaming, fear and ridicule turn students away from trust in what they intuitively know. And approval, the number one seducer of young minds and hearts, works to convince students that they don't know what they know. "See it our way and you'll have instant approval." "Believe what we believe and our approval is yours now." "Embrace our ideas, follow our rules, obey and you'll have approval without end."

Self-referencing, applying your own yardstick, developing your own ethics, and creating a personal vision of truth win little approval from many in positions of authority. Disapproval is more often the reaction one gets for thinking for one's self.

Allison, a third-grader in her second day of the new school year, was playing outside during noon recess when the line-up bell rang. As she moved in the direction of her assigned line-up spot against the wall on the north end of the building, she spotted her younger brother Geoffrey. Geoffrey, in his second day of afternoon kindergarten, was lining up with the first-graders. That line would take him down the far hall and away from his new classroom.

Allison immediately began to jog across the playground to inform her brother of the correct line-up spot for kindergartners. She was stopped by the adult on duty, who told her to get back in the third-grade line.

"I need to talk to my brother," Allison explained.

"You're in third grade, and third-graders belong over there along the wall."

"But you don't understand. My brother is in the wrong line."

"Your job is to take care of yourself, not your brother. And you belong over by the wall."

"I need to talk to my brother. It will only take a minute."

"If you don't do what I tell you right now and line up by the wall, I'm writing you up for insubordination," the supervising adult told her.

The eight-year-old girl stopped, thought about her choices and the probable consequences for a moment, and then proceeded where her inner guidance directed. She went to her brother and gave him the information he needed to get in the correct line. Allison then went immediately to her assigned line-up spot and waited for the bell that would signal time to return to classrooms.

Later that night, Allison's parents got a call from the school principal telling them that Allison had been written up for insubordination. It seemed she had defied a direct order of a playground supervisor.

"Low in responsibility" is a way this child could be perceived by school personnel. In reality, her actions were the essence of self-responsibility. Allison knew what would happen if she did and what would happen if she didn't talk to her brother. She thought about her options, made a clear choice, and accepted the consequences of her choice. Her behavior represents the height of self-responsibility.

What is it like to be a young child attempting to listen to inner guidance while real world authority pressures you to do otherwise? What kind of strength does it take to ignore rules because your insides are telling you rules are situational and this situation doesn't fit this rule? What must it be like to get no reward—in fact only punishment—for standing by your own convictions? If you're not sure, why not check it out inside? Your answer may be there.

Ask yourself these questions: Is obedience a goal of education—or is thinking for yourself? Do we want students that mind—or students who consider circumstances and decide on their own? Do we want students who create their own personal truths—or students who follow the path to ours? Do we want children that adhere to a code of ethics—or students who observe a stringent set of rules?

There is a part of you that knows the answers to these questions. Is it the part that has been trained to look to university professors, textbooks, boards of education or the school administration for guidance? Or is it the part that has learned to look within—to touch a deeper knowing?

Spirit Whisperers put the Principle of Inner Knowing to use in their own lives. They have developed the ability to create their own truths, to find their own wisdom. They know what they know. Their classrooms and the learning experiences they structure reflect that knowing. Because they live it, they can offer it to others.

Schools need fewer rules and more guidelines or class norms for students to live by. A set of principles called "Responsible Action Statements" replace rules in some Spirit Whisperers' classrooms. Responsible Action Statements provide guidelines, point   direction, and give students something to think about as they interact in the classroom.

Here are one teacher's Responsible Action Statements.

1.   Mistakes are permitted here.
2.   All behavior equals a choice.
3.   Problems can be seen as opportunities.
4.   Speaking up for yourself is responsible.
5.   Each person decides the degree of risk to take.
6.   In-sight comes from within.

Responsible Action Statements do not tell students what to do. They provide a framework for discussion from which individual ethics can evolve. They reflect the concept that authentic authority cannot be found outside of yourself and is the only authority you carry with you wherever you go.

Spirit Whisperers direct their gift of guidance toward inner discipline and inner knowing. They have become pioneers of in-sight, helping others to touch and trust that wise part within. Their desire is to bring out what already exists in students and help them use it in line with the concept described in the next chapter, "The Principle of Conscious Creation."

CHAPTER 3

The Principle of Conscious Creation

"I don't know what to do about the school election," Patrick wrote in his language arts journal. "Most people are voting for Allie because she's popular and on the volleyball team. Jo Anne asked me to make some posters for her. She's been nice to me, but all my friends think she's a dork. I'm stuck between a rock and a hard place." Patrick's teacher wrote back, "A more helpful question to ask yourself in this situation might be, 'Who do I want to be in this situation?' Ask yourself that question and see what comes up for you."

Patrick's teacher's response to his journal entry flows out of her belief that the classroom is not primarily a place of discovery. Like other Spirit Whisperers, this teacher has asked herself whether she sees her classroom as a center for debate, a spawning ground of inquiry, or as an environment arranged to be conducive to learning. Although her classroom can be all of those things from time to time, she sees it, first and foremost, as a place of creation.

While students are learning to write in cursive, while they're exploring explorers, while they're constructing a clay sculpture, while they're solving a page full of fraction problems, while they're completing any of the content tasks assigned to them, they are simultaneously in the process of creation. Not the creation of answers to math problems, or of a clay sculpture, or of a full page of penmanship, but the creation of something far more important than the subject matter assignment on which they are working. Minute by minute, day by day, whether they know it or not, students are creating who and what they are.

Every decision a student makes helps define who he or she is. Self-creation occurs and self-definition is announced with everything he or she does. All acts express to the world how he sees himself and give visibility to the person he thinks he is. The kind of clothes she wears, the friends she chooses, the effort she puts into a spelling test, the questions she asks are all acts of creation. So is the music he listens to, the language she uses, and the responses he or she makes to unexpected events that show up in their life.

THE CREATION TRILOGY

Spirit Whisperers are invested in making the process of creation conscious for their students. To do that they work to keep students awake—awake to the fact that they are constantly creating who and what they are. To Spirit Whisperers, that creation is more important than any product constructed at any time by any child in the teacher's classroom.

Students create themselves by making decisions in three areas—what we might call "the creation trilogy." Self-creation involves making conscious choices in three areas: behavior, thoughts, and words.

BEHAVIOR

Many students are sleepwalking through their lives. They behave much like an ostrich, the universal symbol of unconsciousness. Warmth and comfort can come from sticking one's head in the sand. Yet, when your head is safely and securely underground, another piece of your anatomy becomes prominently exposed and vulnerable.

Many students live their lives similar to another animal that can represent unconsciousness—the cow. A cow wakes up in the morning, walks out of the barn, strolls into the pasture, sees a clump of grass beneath its feet, and eats it. Then it spots another clump of grass and eats that one. Then it sees another one and eats again. The cow goes through many repetitions of this process. Finally it looks up. Finding itself on the other side of the pasture, the cow might then say to itself, "Gee, I'm over here. I wonder how I got here." To a cow and to an unconscious student, things just seem to happen. They have no idea how they got where they are. They remain unaware of their choices and unaware of their role in the creation of who and what they are.

The language arts teacher who wrote in the student's journal, "Who do you want to be?" was implementing the Principle of Conscious Creation. She was inviting that student to become aware that his decision about the class election was more than a decision about the class election. That decision was an opportunity to consciously create who he was in relation to the election. She was attempting to help him consciously define himself.

Students sit in your classroom asleep or awake. They are aware or they are not. The Spirit Whisperer's job is to wake up those students that are sleepwalking and help them stay conscious. Reminding students that they are choosing who they are is one way of helping students stay awake.

Staying awake means you choose awareness instead of unconsciousness. Living in a state of awareness means you pay attention to what is happening in your life, what you are doing, and the possible effects of your actions. It means giving up "playing dumb" and pretending you don't know what you know.

Helping students stay conscious and live from awareness is no easy task. Some students don't want to be conscious. They would rather sleepwalk through your class and through their lives. To be awake, they would have to take responsibility for what is happening in their lives, and for many students that prospect is terrifying. It is easier to play victim by pretending they are unaware.

Some students eat unconsciously, bolting down their food without tasting it and reaching for seconds without registering what they're doing. Other students lose friends unconsciously, not noting the effects of their words or actions on others. Some students claim that "time just got away from me," denying the responsibility they have in keeping track of time. "I lost my temper," responds the student who pretends that his temper is somehow separate from the rest of his being.

The awakening process is about increasing students' conscious attention. It is about helping them take notice. We teach five-year-olds to stop, look, and listen before they cross the street. To help students of all ages stay conscious and experience fully what is happening in their lives we need to add "feel" to the equation. Instead of "stop, look, and listen," the saying becomes, "stop, look, listen, and *feel*." If you stop, look, listen, and feel, you are awake. You are living in the moment, consciously. You are expressing the Principle of Conscious Creation.

One way Spirit Whisperers encourage students to stay conscious is by helping them tune into what they are doing in the present moment. They have replaced the familiar teacher lament "*Why* are you doing that?" with "*What* are you doing?"

"Why did you do that?" takes the child's attention off the behavior. Children often hear "Why did you do that?" as "Why did you ever do something so stupid?" and typically activate defensiveness or resistance, which creates a power struggle between the student and the adult. Attention to the original behavior is shoved aside as the student's focus moves away from the behavior to the conflict with the teacher.

Many children simply don't know why they did something. When they don't know, they're not able to communicate why they hit or spit or got angry. Why a child did something is irrelevant anyway. *What* they are doing is more important than *why* they did it.

Carmelle is a fourth-grader who wanders around the room from time to time, even when she's expected to be in her seat. She doesn't do it deliberately. Wandering is not an effort on her part to create a power struggle with her teacher. She is not attempting to push any buttons. She simply goes unconscious and begins to wander. When her teacher asks, "Carmelle, what are you doing?" she regains consciousness. She notices where she is, what she is doing, and returns immediately to her seat. She has the best of intentions and is able to do what is asked of her as long as she stays conscious. Helping her focus on *what* she is doing is more helpful to her than asking her *why* she is doing it.

The path to growth and change is not paved with understanding why things happen. That trail is built on understanding *what* is happening—right here, right now. Therefore, Spirit Whisperers help students become aware of *what* they are presently doing.

I recall observing the debriefing of a cooperative group lesson with a seventh-grade class in a rural Midwest community. During the 30-minute work time, the groups had reached consensus on plans for a poster and had begun construction of their group projects. The teacher saved the last 15 minutes of class time to debrief. One of the debriefing questions he designed and presented to the total class for reflection and discussion was, "On a scale of '1' to '10', how satisfying was working in your groups today?"

The first girl in the first group told the class, "I loved it. This was the best group time I've had all year. I gave it a '10'." The next student, in the same group, said, "I hated it. I gave it a '2'." The teacher sat back and listened as the public conversation between the two group-mates proceeded.

"You gave it a '2'? How could you do that?"

"I hated it."

"How could you hate it?"

"Do you really want to know?"

"Yeah, I want to know."

"Okay, I'll tell you. I hated it because you got to talk all the time. I hardly got to say anything. I made two suggestions and you didn't write either one of them down. You seemed more interested in your ideas. So after a while I just sat there. Not much fun for me."

"Oh."

The girl who had done most of the talking in the group was not aware of her behavior. She was also unconscious of how her behavior was affecting other group members. One of the major benefits of debriefing (detailed in Chapter 2) is that it makes behaviors conscious.

"What prevented your group from getting started quickly?" is a debriefing question that helps students tune into the behaviors they used to prevent a quick start. "List five encouraging things that were said in your group today" invites students to pay attention to encouragement. It makes the encouragement that was present visible. It makes it conscious. "What factors contributed to your government grade?" and "Which factor did you have the most control over?" are questions that increase awareness. They are designed to gently shake the student into wakefulness.

Other debriefing questions/statements that help students stay conscious include:

1. WHAT DID YOU NOTICE ABOUT YOUR BODY LANGUAGE BEFORE AND AFTER YOU LISTENED WITH RESPECT?

2. IN YOUR OPINION, WAS THE INFORMATION I PROVIDED ON BUS BEHAVIOR ACCURATE? EXPLAIN YOUR ANSWER.

3. WHAT PROCEDURES DID YOU FOLLOW TO MAKE SURE EVERYONE IN YOUR GROUP FELT INCLUDED?

4. WHAT WAS THE MOST SELF-RESPONSIBLE BEHAVIOR YOU CHOSE ON THE FIELD TRIP?

5. LIST THE GOOD THINGS THAT HAPPENED BECAUSE WE GOT STARTED QUICKLY.

6. IN TERMS OF IGNORING DISTRACTIONS, I THINK OUR CLASS IS
   - getting better
   - staying the same
   - getting worse
   EXPLAIN YOUR ANSWER IN TWO SENTENCES OR LESS.

7. LIST THREE THINGS YOU DID TODAY TO FOLLOW OUR CLASS CREED. LIST THREE THINGS YOU SAW OTHERS DO TO FOLLOW OUR CLASS CREED.

8. WHAT WAS THE BIGGEST HURDLE YOU HAD TO GET OVER TO REACH AGREEMENT WITH YOUR PARTNER? HOW DID YOU DO THAT?

9. WHAT ARE THINGS WE CAN DO TO LEAVE THE LUNCHROOM CLEANER TOMORROW? WHAT IS ONE THING THAT WILL HELP YOU REMEMBER?

10. WHAT FACTORS CONTRIBUTED TO THE EFFECTIVE TRANSITION YOU JUST MADE FROM LANGUAGE ARTS TO MATH?
11. WHAT EVIDENCE DID YOU HEAR THAT YOUR GROUP WAS KEEPING TRACK OF TIME?
12. HOW DID IT FEEL TO BE INVITED TO PARTICIPATE? HOW DID IT FEEL TO INVITE OTHERS TO PARTICIPATE?
13. MY DEGREE OF LISTENING AT THE ASSEMBLY TODAY WAS:

0 1 2 3 4 5 6 7 8 9 10
LOW   MODERATE   HIGH

14. HOW CLOSE DID YOU COME TO ACHIEVING YOUR POINT GOAL ON THE MATH TEST? WHAT DO YOU ATTRIBUTE THAT TO?
15. WHAT PATTERN DO YOU SEE REGARDING YOUR EFFORTS TO PREPARE FOR THE FIRST THREE SPELLING TESTS?

Increased student consciousness is a goal of Spirit Whisperers. By waking students up—by expanding their awareness—we put them more at choice. Awareness does not guarantee the student will make a different choice. By itself, awareness does not produce change. Awareness only presents the student with choice and the opportunity to change.

If I'm chewing ice in the movie theatre and am unaware of the effect my crunching has on those around me, I will maintain my present behavior. If someone sitting behind me informs me politely that the ice crunching is distracting to her and preventing her from enjoying the movie, being the mature, sophisticated adult that I am, I will alter my behavior. The awareness of the effect of my behavior puts me at choice. Consciousness doesn't *make* my choice. It *permits* my choice.

If a child doesn't know what he is doing, how will he ever do anything different? If a student doesn't know what is going on, he will likely keep it on-going. School, learning, and life in general rarely work for young people who don't know what is going on. Part of your job is to wake students up and keep them alert to their "goings on" in your classroom.

Again, just because a student knows what is going on doesn't mean she will alter her behavior. She may continue to keep on keeping on. Regardless, awareness has its impact. Increasing student awareness is a lot like spitting in someone's soup. If the other person is aware that you just spit in their soup, they may go ahead and eat the soup anyway, but it won't taste quite the same. Once awareness is increased, it cannot return to its original form. Awareness does not contract. Awareness can be distorted, but it cannot be diminished.

Conscious awareness is possible with students in all grade levels. Kindergartners can become aware of the degree of whine in their voices, fourth-graders can become conscious of their use of sarcasm, middle-schoolers can tune into the volume of their conversations, and high-schoolers can become aware of put-downs. An eleven-year-old and an eleventh-grader can be conscious of giving up. A five-year-old and a fifth-year senior can heighten their awareness of the degree of concentration they bring to a task.

A fifth-grade teacher from the Southwest began an exercise in teaching her students about concentration with the words, "I want everyone to find an object in the room to focus on for a moment. When I give the signal to begin, I want you to give the object your full attention. I want you to concentrate on it for 10 seconds. Okay, begin."

After 10 seconds the teacher said, "Stop. Now *unfocus.* Just let your mind wander for a while without thinking of your object or anything in particular." After a few seconds she continued, "Now, focus on the object again, this time for 20 seconds. Give it your full attention. Bring your power of concentration to it."

When the 20 seconds were up, she said, "Okay, stop. Unfocus again. Relax your concentration." She paused for a moment. "Now, make a spyglass with your hands." The teacher demonstrated by making two fists, putting them together and then up to her eye. She modeled the behavior she wanted from her students by looking through her fists at an object across the room. "Now, look at your object with your spyglass. Focus it by adjusting your hands back and forth. Focus on your object for 20 seconds. Bring it into sharp view with your spyglass."

When the students had completed her instructions, the teacher said, "Okay, stop and put your spyglass down. Unfocus for a few seconds."

"Now," she continued a few moments later, "use your power to focus again, using binoculars." She made two "okay" signs with her hands and put them up to her eyes to demonstrate. Students followed suit. "Now look through your binoculars at your object. Concentrate on it again for a few seconds."

She repeated the process. "Once again, stop and unfocus. Relax. Let your mind wander." Then she gave further instructions. "This time I want you to put blinders on—the way we use blinders with horses to help them concentrate and ignore distractions." Again, she demonstrated by using her hands, holding them up to the sides of her face to simulate blinders. "With your blinders, focus on your object one last time. Begin."

"Okay, stop," she said, a few seconds later. "Let me tell you why I asked you to do this last activity. Each of you has the power to focus or unfocus. You can use that power at any time in this class," she assured her students. "It's called 'concentration,' and it is within your power to activate or deactivate. You now know what it feels like to concentrate, and you also know how lack of concentration feels. You can tell when your concentration is turned up and you can tell when it is turned down. You also know *who* turns it up and down. Once you become aware of your level of concentration, you can choose to alter it in any way you see fit, depending on your purpose.

"We'll have some spot checks throughout the day. Every once in awhile I'll stop and ask you to do a concentration check. Your job will be to decide how well you were concentrating on the activity you were doing at the time. I'll also ask you how aware you were of that degree of concentration. My goal is to help you become aware of your awareness level. So pay attention to your level of attention today. Watch yourself and see what you're deciding to do with your concentration."

Encouraging students to notice what they are doing— that's the business of Spirit Whisperers. Many students don't know what they are doing. If a student doesn't know what she is doing, she is powerless to change that doing.

Helping students notice what they're doing develops the silent witness within them. It is our silent witness that allows us to take a step back, leave automatic pilot, and live consciously. Automatic behavior ceases being automatic when we notice it. Students may still choose the same behavior when they become conscious, but at least their choice is conscious.

The act of witnessing removes a behavior from the unconscious and adds it to consciousness. This puts the child at choice, an empowering procedure discussed in detail in Chapter 5, "The Principle of Personal Power." Being at choice, the student can live from intention. He or she can now live deliberately, purposefully creating who he or she wants to be. Creation can come from acting consciously or from reacting unconsciously. To take charge of that creation and have it happen purposefully, a student must stay conscious. This is the essence of the Principle of Conscious Creation.

THOUGHTS

Awareness of behavior is the first aspect of the creation trilogy through which we employ the Principle of Conscious Creation. As Spirit Whisperers, we must also help students stay conscious of the second aspect: thought.

Imagine that you're a passenger boarding a train. Your intention is to travel from Chicago to New York. You climb the stairs, stow your luggage, and quickly fall asleep to the sounds of the track beneath the wheels. After a lengthy nap you awake to the conversation of fellow passengers describing what they'll be doing when they arrive in St. Louis. A quick reality check provides startling information. You're on a train headed west. But since you want to go to New York, your intended destination is obviously east.

How do you react? What do you do now? If you're like most people, you disembark at the next stop and seek out a train going in your intended direction. The transportation decision in this instance is basic. Since you don't like where you're headed, you arrange for transportation that will take you in the appropriate direction.

Spirit Whisperers understand this concept and use it with their most valuable transportation system, their train of thought. They realize that creation begins with thoughts and that destinations and outcomes can be altered dramatically by changing the direction of those thoughts.

Right now, as you read this, your train of thought is moving you toward a destination. By monitoring your thought process and making your thoughts conscious, you can take active control of those thoughts and positively influence their direction and your destination.

If your thought train is loaded with negative thinking, separating emotions, and judgmental cargo, your destination is likely to be unhappiness, depression, or impaired relationships with students and peers. On the other hand, if your train of thought carries faith, appreciation, love, and forgiveness, a happy destination of energy, joy, fulfilling professional practice, and meaningful relationships is created.

We create our own reality, and that process begins with the thoughts we choose to think. Thoughts are first cause. Whether we are conscious of them or not, our thoughts produce outcomes in our lives.

Making thoughts conscious is the first step in taking charge of the direction of your life. If you get on a train of thought that is headed in an unproductive direction, you can change trains. You can get off anywhere along the line and change your destination. Take charge of the thoughts you put in your mind and you take charge of your life.

Spirit Whisperers teach students to appreciate the notion of thoughts as cause. Remember the story line of *The Little Engine That Could*? The little engine's primary thought was "I think I can. I think I can. I think I can." And the destination turned out to be accomplishment and success.

I watched and listened recently as a teacher used this book with her students. Her class sat and listened intently as she read with great expression of the little engine's struggle. Following the story, this teacher led a discussion, invited journal writing, and assigned a personal response paper to be completed and turned in later in the week.

As you read the preceding paragraph, did you imagine the teacher reading in an early childhood classroom? This scene did not unfold in a preschool, kindergarten, or first-grade classroom. It happened in a high school English class and was organized by a teacher who believes important literature can arrive in all kinds of packages, picture books included.

The Little Engine That Could can help high-schoolers as well as young children learn the concept that each person controls his or her own thoughts. That's where a student's power lies and where creation of his life begins. No one can make anyone else think a thought. Each person is the engineer on his own train of thought. Each child lays her own track in a direction of her own choosing. Each creates daily the flow of her life by the thoughts she chooses to think.

Spirit Whisperers believe that teaching a student the cause-and-effect relationship between thoughts and outcomes is more important than understanding the periodic table, knowing the definition of a circle, or discussing the reasons Magellan came to the New World. They realize that once a child grasps the throttle of his train of thought and actively experiences the power that comes from providing direction for his own life, there is no destination that is unavailable to that child. When that happens, a Spirit Whisperer has indeed touched a child's spirit.

Each of you has within you the ability to teach your students about the power of thought. The question is, will you invest the time and energy toward that end?

Be aware of your thoughts right now. Do a quick thought check on yourself. Are you thinking, "That's impossible; I could never do that"? Or are your thoughts more along the lines of "I want this for my students, now"? Many thought reactions are possible, including:

- "My principal wouldn't like me doing that."
- "I'm an algebra teacher. This doesn't apply to me."
- "I'll find a way to begin Monday."
- "I am a Spirit Whisperer. I will do this."
- "If I did this my colleagues would think I was crazy."
- "Parents would complain."
- "I don't have tenure yet. This is too risky."
- "I can't even control my own thoughts. How would I ever teach this to third-graders?"

- "This feels right to me. I'm going to trust my intuition."
- "If I teach this to my students, it will help me do it in my own life."

Whether or not the thoughts you're having right now are similar to any of these is unimportant. What is significant is that whatever those thoughts are they're leading you in a specific direction. They are on course to delivering you to a destination. Is the destination you're heading toward the destination of your choosing? Are your thoughts pointing you in the direction you want to go? If not, change them, and you will alter your life.

LANGUAGE

The third piece of the creation trilogy that Spirit Whisperers teach is the importance of the spoken word. Words are much more than a medium of communication. Words are a medium of perception. The words you use affect how you perceive the world. They help create your beliefs, and they influence your actions.

Words are the tools that program our biocomputers. They affect our hearts and our minds. Spirit Whisperers understand that there is a connection between the words we use, the beliefs we hold, and the actions we take. They realize they can get the Principle of Conscious Creation working in their lives by purposefully selecting words and language patterns that get them where they want to be.

Spirit Whisperers teach students the power of language. I'm not talking about development of an extensive vocabulary, using contractions correctly, or learning the relationship between adverbs and verbs. Correct capitalization, punctuation, and syllabification are not a part of this teaching either. Although Spirit Whisperers teach students the correct use of English and foreign languages, this teaching goes beyond mechanics. It teaches students how to speak with self-responsible language.

Self-responsible language, which is explained in detail in one of my earlier books, *Talk Sense to Yourself: Language and Personal Power*, is comprised of words, phrases, and sentences that show ownership for the effects one creates. This kind of language communicates an acceptance of responsibility for one's actions and feelings. It reveals consciousness, choice, and unlimited potential. Examples include:

- "I chose to turn it in late." (consciousness, choice and ownership)
- "I can do that. I'll give it a shot." (unlimited potential)
- "I don't like the outcome I produced." (ownership)
- "I was in the office because I used inappropriate language." (consciousness and acceptance of responsibility)
- "I decided to be polite and it worked." (consciousness and choice)
- "My preparation really paid off on that test." (ownership)
- "I don't like it when you mark on my paper. I'm frustrated." (ownership)

Language can also disown responsibility for one's actions and feelings. This kind of language communicates unconsciousness and places responsibility on someone or something outside of one's self. It creates boundaries and constricts possibilities. Examples of unconscious language include:

- "He made me mad." (disowns responsibility)
- "I can't do it." (creates boundaries)
- "I'm too short (tall, old, young, uncoordinated, muscle-bound)." (creates boundaries, constricts possibilities)
- "It wasn't my fault." (disowns responsibility)

- "I got carried away." (unconsciousness)
- "That's just the way I am." (limits possibilities)
- "The anger just came over me." (unconsciousness, disowning responsibility)

The ultimate disowning statement was uttered by the student who threw the first punch in a high school fight that resulted in 13 suspensions, 2 broken noses, and 27 stitches. When asked by the principal how come he launched the first blow, the student replied matter-of-factly, "He looked at me."

The importance of self-responsible language shows up in the outcomes that flow from it. It takes self-responsible words and self-responsible language to think self-responsible thoughts. This is similar to the notion that it takes positive words to think positive thoughts. Ever try to think positive thoughts using negative words? It doesn't work. Neither does using disowning language in an attempt to think self-responsible thoughts.

Self-responsible thoughts, particularly those that we repetitiously say to ourselves, become our beliefs. Likewise, those disowning thoughts that we think over and over again become our beliefs. If you repeatedly think the thought, "He's making me mad," you'll begin to believe other people can make you mad. If you repeatedly think of yourself as a klutz, you'll begin to believe that you're a klutz.

So it takes self-responsible words to think self-responsible thoughts. And repetitious thoughts become our beliefs. The final step in this language application of the Principle of Conscious Creation is recognizing that our behavior flows out of our beliefs.

If I believe I can, I choose different behaviors than if I believe I can't. If I believe I'm a fast learner, I act differently than if I believe I'm a slow learner. If I believe I'm a klutz, I approach certain tasks differently than if I believe I'm coordinated.

The point is, if we want self-responsible behaviors from our students, one way to get there is to help them learn self-responsible language.

All educators are responsible for helping students use language correctly. All of us are responsible for building vocabulary, improving spelling, and decreasing grammatical errors. Spirit Whisperers take that responsibility one step further and extend their efforts to include teaching the language of responsibility.

Spirit Whisperers help students remain conscious of how they talk, how they think, and how they behave. They put the thought, word, and deed trio to work helping students consciously create who and what they are.

Karen Strudle is a ten-year teaching veteran. She feels her first responsibility is to help high school students learn and appreciate history. She believes in the importance of her subject and often jokes that she refers to it as "subject matter" because her subject is the only one that really matters. Karen believes that without a firm grounding in the events that have led our society to where it is today, we are doomed to repeat the mistakes of the past as well as to ignore the mistakes of the present. "You have to have history lessons if you're going to learn the lessons of history," she preaches throughout each semester.

Even though Karen teaches history with a passion, she never loses sight of the fact that she also teaches children. Maybe that's why in the middle of history lessons she stops and implements activities like The "Be" Choice.

"I'm going to allow 30 seconds," she informed her history students during one class period in the middle of the year, "and your assignment is to look around the room. Just gaze about and do whatever comes naturally until I call time." When the time was up, Karen invited her students to record their reactions and their experience on paper.

With the writing completed, Karen explained the difference between a "do" choice and a "be" choice. "We all make 'do' choices in our lives," she began. "We decide to do our homework, make a phone call, go to the mall, shoot baskets, buy a new shirt, clean our room, wash the car. All of us are familiar with making 'do' choices. Some of us even have 'To do' lists and cross off each item as we complete it.

"Less often we make 'be' choices. A 'be' choice is a decision we make about how to 'be' when we do whatever it is that we 'do.' For instance, I might decide to eat out tonight. Going out for dinner is my 'do' choice. That's what I plan to do tonight. While I'm doing that activity, I could choose to 'be' several different ways. I could choose to be adventurous and risk eating some new meal that I haven't yet experienced. I could choose to be frugal and look over the menu for the best bargain. Another way I could be is friendly. Having made that decision, I would initiate conversations with others, smile at the server, and act pleasant and interested with my dinner partner. Or I could choose to be harried and make a real effort to get in and out of the restaurant as soon as possible. How I choose to 'be' will greatly affect how I experience what I choose to 'do.'

"I'm going to ask you again to look around the room. Only this time, before you do that, I want you to make a 'be' choice. You could choose to be curious, bored, friendly, tired, alert, interested, excited, humorous, thorough, critical, appreciative, or any other 'be' choice you can think of. So make a 'be' choice now and write it on your paper."

When her students had finished writing, Karen said, "Okay, now look around the room for 30 seconds, 'being' the way you chose. Begin."

After their second look-around, this veteran history teacher asked students if they had noticed any differences or similarities between the first and second look-around periods. Comments were offered in abundance.

- "I picked 'thorough' as my 'be' choice, and I noticed much more detail the second time."
- "I decided to be playful and I couldn't stop myself from smiling. I never smiled once the first time."
- "I was much more relaxed the second time. The first time I was trying to guess what you were going to ask us when we were done so I tried to memorize everything I saw. The second time was a lot different because I chose to be disinterested."

To bring closure to this part of the lesson, Karen summarized: "So most of you had a different experience each time, even though the 'do' part remained the same. I think we can conclude from your comments that how we choose to 'be' is pretty important to the outcome of an activity, even one as simple as looking around the room for 30 seconds.

"Imagine applying this notion to other, more important tasks like babysitting, taking a test, going to an assembly, calling a friend, or driving a car. Think of how this choice would alter your experience of being in this class. In fact, what are some ways you could choose to 'be' here in history class?"

Responses came quickly.

- "Excited."
- "Interested."
- "Bored."
- "Attentive."
- "Tired."
- "Alert."
- "Curious."
- "Respectful."
- "Distracting."

"Yes, you could make any of those choices here," Karen concluded. "And each would alter your experience of this class. You have a lot of power here, class. This is personal power that you can access or let go sliding by. You can't always control what you 'do' here. I get to make many of those decisions. But you can always control how you choose to 'be' here. That decision is always under your control.

"I want to challenge all of you right now to make a 'be' choice every time you walk through this classroom door for the rest of this week. See if you can stay conscious of your 'be' choice and 'be' that way for the entire period. We'll stop and talk about this notion occasionally this week. Make a 'be' choice now, for the rest of this period. Write it on your assignment sheet and keep it in front of you. I'll do the same and write mine on the board so you can see my choice."

I don't know the "be" choice that Karen Strudle made for the remainder of that hour. But I do know that somewhere along the road of becoming a professional educator, she chose to be a Spirit Whisperer.

Being gives birth to doing. In order to experience yourself as being excited, you must do something that demonstrates excitement. To be caring, you must perform caring acts. To be thoughtful, it is necessary to think some thoughts. To be focused, you must perform behaviors that initiate and maintain focus.

In order to experience yourself as being respectful, it is necessary to do respectful things. Feeling respectful is not enough. Thinking of yourself as respectful is not enough. You could feel respect for another person from the top of your head all the way down to your toes, but if you perform no behaviors that demonstrate respect, you are not being respectful.

If I feel love but don't do anything loving, is that love? If I feel generous, but perform no act of generosity, am I being generous? I may *feel* loving and generous, but I don't get to *experience* myself as being loving and generous unless I perform loving and generous behaviors.

Word, thought, deed, and being all lead to creation. So does perception. Spirit Whisperers also help students focus on their perceptions as a way of inviting them to experience the Principle of Conscious Creation.

Spirit Whisperers realize that perception is a choice. Whereas you can't always control the events of your life, you can always control how you see those events.

Sometimes things get spilled in classrooms. Paint, milk, pins, water, even chemicals get spilled on occasion. Of course we attempt to control for spillage. A classroom spill, whatever the variety, is an event that most of us would like to keep to a minimum. So we use low, flat containers to control for spillage. We keep caps on liquids. We have specific places for things. We teach students how to use materials appropriately and safely so spills are less like to occur. But regardless of our efforts to eliminate spills, spills happen.

While you cannot totally control whether or not paint gets spilled in your classroom, you do have control over how you perceive that spill. Some teachers see spilled paint as awful—a catastrophe. Others see spilled paint as an opportunity—a chance to help students learn about cooperation or cleanup. Some see it as a nuisance. Others see it as a signal that debriefing is called for.

Spilled paint is not good or bad. It is just spilled paint. It only becomes good, bad, a nuisance, a signal, an opportunity, or a catastrophe once we choose how to see it. Since spilled paint can be viewed in a variety of ways, how we see it tells more about us than it does about the paint. It tells how we are choosing to see. It tells how we choose to have the event we call "spilled paint" be for us.

Behaviors can flow from perceptions. If I see spilled paint as awful, I am more likely to implement behaviors that reflect blame and punishment. I assign blame, find fault, and hand out punishments. I reprimand individuals, remove painting as a privilege from some, raise my voice and act angry.

On the other hand, if I see spilled paint as an opportunity, I use that opportunity to model the search for solutions and am more likely to implement solution-seeking behaviors. I teach students the behaviors that are necessary for solving the immediate problem of spilled paint. Later, I lead them through a solution-seeking process designed to elicit preventative solutions.

Spirit Whisperers realize that since perception is a choice, how they see a classroom crisis is yet another way to define who they are. All events present themselves as opportunities to choose who we are. Spilled paint is no exception. Spilled paint is a gift presented to us by our students—a gift that places us in a position where we must decide if we want to be a solution-seeker or a punisher.

A third-grader gets to decide how to see teasing by classmates. An eighth-grader chooses how to perceive put-downs. A basketball player decides how to view the recent defeat. Students choose the perception they bring to bombing a test, in-school suspension, or making the honor roll. As these events occur, a conscious student observes them and decides who she is in relation to them. Again, she gets to decide what perception to bring to them, to choose who she wants to be.

Spirit Whisperers teach students that if painful events, unsatisfying conditions, or frustrations show up in their lives, they can work to change the event or change the way they perceive it. Students can learn to positively confront the student who teases and puts them down. They can communicate assertively, stating, "That sounds like a put-down. It hurts. I wish you would choose a different way to talk to me." Working to alter the event is sometimes effective. Other times it is not.

When activating behaviors designed to change events is nonproductive, students can change how they choose to see those events. They can change their inner experience of the event. They can change their thoughts about it, how they perceive it, and their internal reaction to it. When students receive a put-down they can say to themselves, "She must be having a bad day," or "This isn't about me. This is about where he is today." The student can choose to perceive the person sending put-downs as feeling powerless and small rather than viewing them as big and intimidating.

Students can learn that what they see depends on how they see it. They can learn they have choices in what they see in any situation. As students learn that perception is a choice, they are empowered to put the Principle of Conscious Creation to work in their lives.

A student who lives in tune with the Principle of Conscious Creation lives his life by choice; a student who lives unconsciously, without purposefully creating, lives a life of chance. Spirit Whisperers invite students to awaken to the awareness of choice and, if they so choose, live consciously. They allow students to assume responsibility for that choice and, in so doing, begin to activate the Principle of Personal Responsibility, the subject of the next chapter.

CHAPTER 4

The Principle of Personal Responsibility

- "He hit me first."
- "She ripped my coat."
- "The substitute didn't follow our class routines."
- "I couldn't help it."
- "The assembly ran over time."
- "The ref was blind."
- "He didn't ask the right questions on the test."

Although each of these comments speaks to a different situation, each represents a student playing the game of life from the position of victim.

Victims work hard. They work hard to disown responsibility for what happens in their lives. They work hard to convince you that others are to blame or at fault. They work hard to manipulate others into doing things for them. They work hard to wiggle out of responsibility that belongs to them.

Spirit Whisperers also work hard. They work hard to combat the victim mentality that surfaces in their students by taking responsibility for putting the Principle of Personal Responsibility to work in their classrooms.

Victims attribute events, situations and results that show up in their lives to chance, luck, circumstance, or something or someone outside of their control. "I was in the wrong place at the wrong time," they say, disowning responsibility for being there in the first place. "She threw one at me first" is the explanation they offer in an attempt to duck the role they played in the melee. "We got home late," they use to explain their choice of not finishing a homework assignment.

A key phrase that Spirit Whisperers employ to help students focus on the role they play in creating results in their lives is, "What do you attribute that to?" This phrase is an effort to help students experience what Albert Schweitzer meant when he said, "The man who succeeds consistently is the man who in all experiences looks for the ultimate cause of things in himself."

"What do you attribute that to?" and similar Teacher Talk language is an attempt to help students hear and feel the connection between their efforts (cause) and the results that follow (effect). Teacher Talk that focuses students on their own efforts, actions, energy, choices, and attitudes helps them take personal responsibility for the results they create.

- "So you got suspended. [effect] What do you attribute that to?" [cause]
- "No time-outs today. [effect] How did you create that result?" [cause]
- "I'm wondering how you pulled off [cause] that 'A' in science." [effect]
- "What did you do [cause] to get finished on time?" [effect]
- "What steps did you take [cause] to learn how to use the computer?" [effect]

In addition to using language that helps students see the connection between cause and effect, Spirit Whisperers use activities to increase students' *attribute awareness*. Attribute awareness, taught in the Performance Learning Systems course, Successful Teaching for Acceptance of Responsibility™, is the degree of awareness a student has of the attributes he or she chooses to bring to bear on a specific situation. This awareness can be heightened by designing and using strategies that help students see and feel the role they play in creating their own experience. That's exactly what a second-grade teacher did when she designed an erasable cause-and-effect display board to use with her students.

CAUSE AND EFFECT

I CHOSE . . .   **RESULT**

This early childhood educator used the display board whenever she heard disowning language or wanted to help students take responsibility for their efforts or the results they produced. One application occurred after two seven-year-olds argued over rules of a flash card game. As she listened to their explanations of the situation, this teacher paraphrased their words and filled in the chart, giving visibility to the relationship between cause and effect.

I CHOSE . . .	RESULT
I chose to get mad.	He got mad.
I chose to rip a card.	I got in trouble.
I chose to say a bad word.	He threw the cards at me.
I chose to throw the cards at him.	I got in trouble, too.

A fifth-grade teacher designed an attribute awareness activity to accompany his return of written reports on endangered species. "Take a minute to look at your grade and read the comments I wrote on each of your reports," he began. "See if you agree with it or not. I want you to look at your grade and make some decisions about how you think that particular grade happened to end up on your paper. I'll distribute a list of several possible factors that may or may not have influenced your grade. Your job is to look at them and decide which factors had the most effect and which ones had the least." The list read:

1.   THE AMOUNT OF TIME I STUDIED
2.   HOW MUCH DETAIL I ADDED TO THE MAIN POINTS
3.   THE KIND OF CLOTHES I WEAR
4.   HOW MUCH THE TEACHER LIKES ME
5.   MY SPELLING ABILITY
6.   THE NEATNESS OF MY HANDWRITING
7.   THE POSITION OF THE STARS IN THE HEAVENS
8.   THE NUMBER OF RESOURCES I USED FOR RESEARCH
9.   THE ATTITUDE I BROUGHT TO THE TASK
10.   THE NUMBER OF TIMES I SMILE IN CLASS

Following distribution of the list, the teacher added further instructions. "Now assign a number to each factor," he said. "Rate them from the most to the least influence they had on your grade." He paused as students followed directions. Discussion of the ratings in small groups followed. A total class discussion brought closure to the activity.

A foreign language teacher helped her students get in touch with attribute awareness as she explained the importance of an upcoming money-raising activity. "The car wash next weekend will help fund our trip to Montreal," she began. "It was the biggest money-maker for last year's class, and I hope we can duplicate their efforts. Let's take a few minutes and explore the talents, skills, and abilities we possess in this class that can be used to help make this project a success. Help me create a list of attributes or factors that we can bring to this activity that will help us."

The class began slowly and then picked up steam as they gradually caught on to what was expected. The final list included:

1.   WE WORK HARD.
2.   WE HAVE MUSCLES.
3.   WE KNOW LOTS OF PEOPLE WITH DIRTY CARS.
4.   WE'RE COMMITTED.
5.   WE KNOW HOW TO ATTRACT ATTENTION.
6.   WE NEED THE MONEY. WE'RE DESPERATE.
7.   THERE ARE A LOT OF US. WE CAN TAKE TURNS.
8.   WE PICKED A GOOD SPOT.
9.   WE CAN PUT POSTERS AROUND THE SCHOOL AND AROUND TOWN.

The French teacher, the early childhood educator who designed the cause-and-effect display board, the teacher who asked his students to determine what caused their grade, and other adults who ask "What do you attribute that to?" are helping students perceive how they create much of what happens in their lives. They are actively implementing the Principle of Personal Responsibility in their classrooms.

I recently invested five months of my life to help raise my grandchildren. While single-parenting Chelsea, age twelve, and Austin, age nine, I exposed them to things about which I care deeply. Horses are one example. Chelsea immediately bonded with my two horses and consistently helped me groom them and clean stalls on our daily visits to the boarding stable. Austin preferred to use that time to jump on the trampoline and play with other children. Both youngsters had opportunities to ride and take lessons from a local instructor.

After three months Chelsea began to show my Arabian gelding at local horse shows. She won ribbons every time out and even captured the blue ribbon on one occasion. After a particularly successful show, a young rider from our stable came up to Chelsea and offered her congratulations. "You're just a natural," the rider said.

On the way home from the show, Chelsea asked me if I thought she was "a natural." I explained to her that I thought she had a talent for riding, but that the results she had created had less to do with being a "natural" and more to do with the hours she had spent in the saddle, the weekly lessons she took, and the seriousness with which she practiced. Her future success and satisfaction depend on attributing her current success to something she has control over—to something she helps create through her own efforts and choices.

Students who feel empowered—who have high self-esteem—attribute things that happen to them to their persistence, degree of study, attitude, effort, energy and commitment. They see the results they produce as something *they* control. They understand the relationship between cause and effect and know that they are the cause and thus control the effect.

Perhaps your students don't believe they are responsible for creating the events that show up in their lives. Then begin by helping them take responsibility for how they respond to those events. The student whose coat gets ripped is responsible for how she responds to that experience. The class that is surprised by the changes in classroom routine made by a substitute teacher is responsible for their reactions to those changes. The athlete who's called "out" when she appears to be "safe" is responsible for her response to the umpire's decision. The youngster who is called names is responsible for his reaction to the name-calling. Many students don't know they are responsible for their reactions to the events in their lives, and their language reveals that lack of awareness.

"He bored me to death sixth hour," the middle school student complains, disowning any responsibility for his reaction to the lecture. "The ump was blind. He cost us the game," whines the student athlete who was ejected following her emotional outburst after a call on a close play. "She got me going," the third-grader remarks, in an effort to blame someone else for his outburst of giggling.

Purposeful use of the words "choose," "decide," and "pick" is one strategy employed by Spirit Whisperers to help students become aware of their responsibility for reactions to events.

- "I see you **chose** to do it over."
- "I noticed you **decided** to use words to express your anger."
- "If you **choose** to keep talking, you'll be **deciding** not to sit by each other for a while."
- "What attitude did you **pick** when the problems got tougher?"
- "So you **chose** to be ejected from the game for your reaction to the call."
- "How did you **choose** to respond when you felt left out?"
- "You **picked** arguing as a way to influence her?"
- "I heard you **chose** control when he teased you."

Repeated use of the words "choose," "decide," and "pick" helps students realize that they are responsible for their reactions to the *what is* of their lives. Follow along in this scenario as a teacher uses effective Teacher Talk to confront a student. Notice how the teacher responds to the child's efforts to deflect responsibility for his actions and reactions.

"I heard you **chose** to end up in the principal's office yesterday."

"Roberto ripped my coat!"

"And how did you **choose** to respond?"

"I can't let him get away with something like that."

"So what behavior did you **pick**?"

"He made me mad!"

"So you **decided** to do what?"

"He started the whole thing."

"And you **chose** to respond with . . .?"

Repetition of this style of language is the key to producing change. I recently presented my full-day Teacher Talk seminar to an elementary school staff near my home. During the presentation I spoke about the importance of using the words "choose," "decide," and "pick." Six weeks later I returned to do a follow-up session designed to debrief the implementation that had occurred during the interim and share additional Teacher Talk strategies.

I got to the school early, set up, and was ready to start before the buses arrived to take the students home on this early dismissal day. I began to wander the building to catch the flavor of the school and perhaps hear some examples of effective Teacher Talk I could use later in my presentation. I was amply rewarded for my efforts.

I entered what I thought was an empty sixth-grade classroom and found the teacher working on lesson plans. Her students were down the hall in physical education class. Our discussion centered on one of her students who was having trouble taking responsibility for his behavior.

This boy fought often, taunted other students, and ended up in the principal's office frequently. In addition, he seldom owned his behavior. According to him, it was always the other person's fault. "He took my ball," "She marked on my paper," "He told lies about me," and—my personal favorite—"He looked at me" were ways he attempted to explain away his responsibility.

This boy was the only constant in the equation. The other student and the situation frequently changed. Although this particular child was present in each of the changing circumstances, in his view he was not responsible.

As we spoke, the student who was the focus of our discussion entered the room. He was alone and had a bloody nose. His previously white Detroit Tiger T-shirt was now mostly red. With a cold paper towel held over his nose, he informed his teacher, "I'm going down to the principal's office. Not sure when I'll be back. I'll come as soon as I can. I just wanted to stop and tell you I chose to get in a fight in the gym today." He then turned on his heels and left.

When he disappeared through the doorway, I gave the teacher a high-five to celebrate. This young man had clearly made a breakthrough. Although he had not yet chosen to refrain from fighting, his language revealed that he was beginning to see himself as a person at choice, as cause, as responsible for his reactions to whatever he felt precipitated that fight. By changing his language from "He made me do it" to "I chose to get in a fight," he is altering his belief system and how he views his place in the events that transpired. In time his behavior will shift to more closely mirror his newly emerging beliefs.

"How did you get that student to talk that way?" I asked his teacher.

"You know how I did it," she teased.

"I know," I confessed, "but I'd like to hear you say it."

"I used those words you taught us at the workshop last time: 'choose,' 'decide,' and 'pick,'" she said, confirming what I already suspected.

"How many times did you use those words?" I asked. "Estimate for me the number of times in the last six weeks you said 'choose,' 'decide,' or 'pick' with him personally or with the whole class where he could hear them. Take a guess."

"About three or four," she began, pausing, then adding special emphasis to her last word, ". . . *hundred*."

Three or four hundred times she used those words with students. Repetition is indeed the key here. Decide to use these words five or six times and they will have little effect. Choose to use them frequently and you increase your chances of favorably impacting your students.

Students who choose to fight and realize they are making a choice have more response-ability than students who don't realize that they are in fact choosing what behavior they wish to manifest. If you're unaware of a choice, you are not as response-able as is someone who is choice conscious.

Victims see little choice in their lives. They often make the same losing response repeatedly. An alcoholic fits this pattern. Problem at home . . . drink. Problem at work . . . drink. Car breaks down . . . drink. Argue with the neighbor . . . drink.

Spirit Whisperers are invested in helping students improve their response-ability. Students who sense more choice in a situation are more likely to come out winners and feel satisfaction. Consider the game of checkers. If you have three kings and your partner has none, you will win. It may take you awhile, but your partner is doomed. Why? You will prevail because kings can move in several directions, covering many spaces at one time. They have more response-ability—a greater ability to respond than an ordinary checker does.

"You always have more choices than you think you have," Spirit Whisperers tell their students, helping them appreciate the fact that a wide variety of responses is available in any given situation. Helping students become aware of meaningful alternatives to their behavior invites them to be response-able and activates the Principle of Personal Responsibility.

Another strategy Spirit Whisperers use to help students become response-able is teaching the desired behavior. Their belief is that if you want a behavior, you have to teach a behavior. "Don't all teachers share that belief?" you may wonder. Probably many teachers do, but not all of them put it into practice.

I recently counseled three middle school teachers who were responsible for 90 seventh-graders. The three teachers team-taught these students and rotated them throughout the day for math, science, language arts, technology, and social studies.

"Their transitions are terrible," one of the frustrated teachers told me. "Once they get settled down they stay on task and work pretty well, but changing from one activity to another or from one classroom to the next is pure chaos."

"Have you taught them how to make an effective transition?" I asked.

"No," the teachers responded in unison.

"Why not?" I probed.

"Because they ought to know how to do that by seventh grade," came the response. The other two heads nodded in agreement.

I agree. These students probably ought to know how to make effective transitions by seventh grade. The point is they don't, as evidenced by their collective behavior. And unless these instructors begin by teaching the specific behaviors they desire, lectures, reprimands, debriefing, and even consequences will have little effect.

A fifth-grade teacher put students into groups of four to compare and contrast two poems. Having the students reach consensus and write up a summary of their findings was also part of her subject matter objective. After explaining to her students what she expected them to do with the content, she moved on to another, equally important part of her lesson.

"I expect some disagreement in your groups today," she informed her students. "Different opinions are likely to surface. Let that be okay. Disagreement is not only allowed, it's encouraged. The disagreement could get you thinking and might even strengthen your final product. It is important that the disagreement be polite, however.

"You have two tasks to work on," she continued. "One is comparing the poems. The other is disagreeing politely. Let's take a minute and explore the 'disagree politely' part of the assignment." The teacher then wrote the words DISAGREE POLITELY on a piece of chart paper and added the words SOUNDS LIKE and LOOKS LIKE under them.

"How will I know if you are disagreeing politely in your groups?" she asked. "What will I hear as I come around and observe today? What does disagreeing politely sound like? Somebody suggest some words. If you choose to disagree politely in your group, how will you say it?"

Students suggested possibilities as the teacher recorded their responses on the chart paper. This is what she recorded:

DISAGREE POLITELY

SOUNDS LIKE   LOOKS LIKE

- "I have a different idea."
- "I'd like to hear some other ideas."
- "That might work. So might . . . "
- "I disagree."

- "I'm not sure that fits."
- "I agree with part of that."
- "You'll have to convince me."

"Yes, those are clearly ways to disagree politely," the teacher said. She then turned her attention to the "looks like" portion of her chart. "While we're disagreeing with words like those we have on our chart, how do we want to look?" she asked. "Let's fill in the 'looks like' side of our chart. How do we want to look so that we communicate our disagreement, but also remain polite?"

Students again offered suggestions.

Looks like

- uncrossed arms
- looking at the person
- lean forward
- stay in own space
- serious look, but friendly

With several items now displayed on each side of the chart, the teacher thanked the students for their input and reviewed the assignments. "Remember, we have two tasks to work on today," she said. "You need to reach consensus on the poems so you can write a summary. While you are doing that, please disagree politely. Both are important. If you work on the poems but don't disagree politely, that's not good enough. If you disagree politely but don't work on the poems, that's not good enough either. Please do both. I'll be coming around to your groups, observing and making notes. We'll talk about how you did on these two tasks later."

A high school technology teacher noticed his students were susceptible to distractions. In the absence of distractions, they worked well, staying on task and completing assignments. The smallest distraction, however, negatively affected time-on-task and task completion for many of his students. Believing that if you want a behavior, you have to teach a behavior, this educator accepted the *isness* of the situation and set out to rectify it.

"Your tech assignment is on the board," he informed his students at the beginning of class one day. "As you can see, it involves reading several pages in your manual and designing a program to fit the specifications that are described on page 78. You will be working independently today to complete this task. It will require strong concentration on your part. As usual, I'll be available for questions or feedback.

"While you're working on designing and implementing the program, I want you to work on one additional task," he explained. "I want you to ignore distractions. I've arranged to have three separate distractions occur sometime during the class period. I'm not going to tell you ahead of time what they are or when they will occur. Your job is to notice them and ignore them, using a five-step process that I'll now explain.

"First, I want you to notice the distraction and silently call it by name. If you see or hear a distraction of any kind, say to yourself, 'There is a distraction.' It's important to notice the distraction because if you're aware of a distraction you have power over it. If you're not aware of it—if you go unconscious—it may have power over you.

"Second, make a decision not to be distracted. This is your point of power. You can claim your power or give it away at this time. I'm asking today that you choose to ignore each distraction.

"The next step is to keep it to yourself. If you notice a distraction, a public announcement is not necessary. Just go about your business without mentioning the distraction to anyone.

"Fourth, refocus. You can refocus a number of ways. You can turn away, cover your ears, pull in closer to your work, re-read the last paragraph, re-read the directions, look at the last thing you entered into your computer, or ask yourself, 'Where am I?' Any of those techniques will help you to refocus.

"Finally, begin again. Just begin on something. Anything."

The technology instructor followed his direct teaching of ignoring distractions by providing the three distractions he promised during the work period. Ten minutes into the lesson he tripped over his chair and knocked several books on the floor. Later, he turned the radio on and loudly played disco music for four minutes. At a quarter after 10 a student recruited from another class opened the door, shouted "Boo!" and ran off down the hall. Debriefing at the end of work time brought closure to an interesting experience and helped students to solidify what they had learned about ignoring distractions and to set goals for next time.

Spirit Whisperers activate the Principle of Personal Responsibility in their classrooms by combining the "If you want a behavior, you have to teach a behavior" philosophy with an equally important stance: that of doing nothing.

Spirit Whisperers believe strongly in the value of doing nothing. It is one of their favorite tools. Spirit Whisperers do nothing for students that students can do or can learn to do for themselves. By doing nothing they do something by giving students room to do things for themselves.

A Spirit Whisperer's job is to give students a system. It's the students' job to use the system. Spirit Whisperers do not run around making sure that students start quickly. They teach their students a system for getting started quickly and allow the students to choose whether or not to use that system. Debriefing the use or lack of use of the system and natural consequences reinforces the teaching of the system.

Rather than create conflict-free classrooms, Spirit Whisperers teach students to disagree politely and help them learn skills to handle the conflict that does occur. They refuse to eliminate all conflict in their classrooms and even welcome differences of opinion as an opportunity to assist their students in learning the skills of handling conflict themselves.

Spirit Whisperers do not give students fish and they refuse to fish for them. Instead, they teach students how to fish and let them decide for themselves whether or not to do any fishing.

What makes students get started quickly, ignore distractions, disagree politely, respect the microscope, share materials, invite participation, and get themselves and others back on task comes from within. We make students victims and support learned helplessness when we take care of them or fail to teach them the skills necessary to take care of themselves.

We also encourage students to take the victim stance when we bail them out, give them one more chance, let them slide, accept excuses, or fail to hold them accountable for the choices they make. When we give up "doing for" students and saving them from their choices, we allow them to take responsibility for their lives. We help them live the Principle of Personal Responsibility.

Are you calling home to get verbal permission when students fail to bring in a permission slip for the field trip? Are you allowing students to call home when they forget their lunch or homework? Are you letting them turn work in late with no consequence if they have a good excuse? If so, you may be rescuing.

Are you reminding students how much time is left in the work period? Do you change group members when students complain about a group-mate? Do you rearrange your seating chart when a student complains that someone is bugging him? If so, you could be rescuing.

There are payoffs to rescuing. Rescuers get to feel good about themselves. They add meaning to their lives by dispensing power in what seems to them to be benevolent and caring ways. They perceive themselves as kind and supportive.

While rescuers often have positive intentions of helping, loving, and serving, what they don't appreciate is that "helping" doesn't always help. Rescuing often breeds learned helplessness. When rescuers take responsibility for victims, they help cement them firmly in the victim position by supporting their victim notions. They rob self-perceived victims of an opportunity to become conscious and to discover what they have created in their own lives.

At some point, we must allow students to take responsibility for themselves. To help them do that we have to get clear on what our responsibility is and what it isn't. Trespass occurs when boundaries are foggy or in transition. Rescuing results from unclear boundaries—from not knowing what responsibility belongs to me and what responsibility belongs to others.

Clear boundaries help make it possible for Spirit Whisperers to invite students to live the Principle of Personal Responsibility. Spirit Whisperers know that it is their responsibility to give students a system and it is the student's responsibility to use the system. Their job is to teach students how to organize a science notebook; it is the student's job to do the organizing. Their responsibility is to teach respect for a guest speaker; the student's responsibility is to demonstrate respect. Their role is to teach students to set priorities and budget time; the student's job is to put those skills to use.

By having and honoring clear boundaries, Spirit Whisperers stay free of codependent, rescuing behavior. They invest their time teaching skills, designing practices where students can use those skills, and debriefing the practices. Their goal is to equip students with skills that will allow them to do for themselves should they so choose.

In spite of Spirit Whisperers' efforts to teach students to get started quickly, organize a science notebook, ignore distractions, and develop similar skills, some students choose not to employ those skills. Spirit Whisperers then turn to their toolbox and choose another tool—one designed to help students come face-to-face with the Principle of Personal Responsibility. That tool is the implementation of consequences.

Spirit Whisperers do not protect students from experiencing the legitimate consequences of their actions. They respect the student's right to choose and support his or her choice by following through with consequences firmly and consistently. Their belief is, if you "consequate," you educate.

Spirit Whisperers use consequences purposefully. They use them to help students appreciate the relationship between cause and effect. They use them so students can see that the choices they make produce results. They use them to motivate students to make responsible decisions. They use them to help students see themselves as capable of making choices and of learning "I created this, therefore I can create that."

Consequences are not used to control, to manipulate, to demonstrate power, or to get even. If you use consequences for purposes of winning or controlling, you have crossed the line and moved away from consequences into the territory called "punishment."

Punishment doesn't work. At best, punishment behaves like Preparation H, providing only temporary relief. A quick glance at our penal system is all that's necessary to reveal the dismal long-term effects of punishment.

Spirit Whisperers believe in holding students accountable for their actions. Consequences, in their opinion, offer a better chance than punishment does for helping students own their behaviors and become response-able.

"Time out," redoing a paper, in-school suspension, creating a plan, an ineligibility slip, missing the field trip, receiving a "D", a call home, or any other action could be a punishment or it could be a consequence. It's not the action you take that determines whether or not it's punishment; it's how you take the action.

Punishment is administered arbitrarily and capriciously. The student rarely knows when it is coming or when it will be enforced. Often the punishment is forced, is unrelated to the behavior, and comes across as retribution. Writing sentences or copying pages from the dictionary for talking out of turn are examples. Having to sit in a time-out area because the teacher finally ran out of patience is another.

Consequences, on the other hand, are natural outcomes, more closely related to the behavior, and are delivered consistently. Students know if they choose to turn a paper in one day late, they are marked down one grade. The consequence happens every time. Students can count on it and plan accordingly. The consequence is simply an outcome that flows naturally from the student's choice.

Punishment is delivered with emphasis on power and authority. The teacher is in charge and is in control of the results. Students are "done to" by others in the position of authority. It becomes someone else's decision if punishment is called for.

It is the students themselves who are in control of whether or not they experience consequences. The emphasis is on cause and effect. Students get to be the cause of what happens to them. They create the results by the choices they make. Therefore, the students have the power and the control.

Students learn more quickly from consequences than they do from punishment. Since they see punishment as something someone else is doing to them, they often activate resistance and resentment in response. Resentment is not a helpful space from which to receive learning. On the other hand, students see consequences as something they have control over, as something they do to themselves. A consequence is more likely to be experienced on the inside because there is no outside force creating the situation.

Punishment demands compliance. Punishment is steadily increased and imposed from the outside until students comply. With consequences, there is no need for students to comply. They are presented with choices that have consequences attached to them. Spirit Whisperers have no preference concerning which choice a student makes. They see a choice to experience negative or positive consequences as an opportunity to help the student learn about cause and effect.

Punishment is often accompanied by anger. The voice sounds threatening and is void of love and caring. The demeanor of the punisher allows the student to focus on the behavior of the punisher rather than encouraging the student to look at himself or at his own behavior. With consequences, the voice communicates respect. Consequences take the negative emotion out of discipline and substitute positive emotions of concern and empathy. Empathy becomes an integral part of the Teacher Talk that announces the consequence. "Bummer, what a shame. I bet that will be a challenge for you now."

Punishment models the search for fault and blame. The adult assumes the roles of detective, police officer, and judge. She gathers the evidence, listens to arguments, sorts through reasons, judges excuses, and makes decisions about guilt and innocence. Considerable time is invested in finding fault and assigning blame. The use of consequences models the search for solutions. The emphasis is on making choices that lead to solutions to the problems that occur. Writing a plan to solve a situation is a typical consequence and becomes the focus of the planning area.

Punishment implies moral judgement and is an effort to lay shame and guilt on the student. "You are wrong" and "You are bad" are the silent messages sent to students through the use of punishment. Punishment often violates the Principle of Suspended Judgement (Chapter 1). Consequences separate the deed from the doer and are void of judgement. The silent message is, "I like you and I don't like the behavior." Students are not made right or wrong and they are held accountable through the use of consequences.

Punishment focuses on past behavior. "Here we go again," "You've been interrupting me all day," and "That's the fifth time this week" are examples of emphasizing the past. Consequences focus on what the student did this time. History plays no part in the implementation of consequences. What happened in the past is over. Next time isn't here yet. The concern is only with the present.

If students choose a behavior that calls for in-school suspension, time-out, or time in the planning room, how you apply that result is what determines whether it's punishment or a consequence. If students know it's coming, if it's delivered consistently, if empathy replaces anger in your voice, if it's set up so that they themselves are clearly the cause, if you hold them accountable without making them wrong, if the goal is to solve the situation so that it doesn't happen again, you have implemented a consequence.

Another clear boundary that Spirit Whisperers honor has to do with ownership of problems. Victims often bring problem situations to an adult in an attempt to get out from under them and turn them over to someone else. All too often rescuers are quick to blur the line between what is the student's problem and what is their (the teacher's) problem. They respond with what they incorrectly feel is a helpful response: giving advice, offering a solution, telling the child what to do, or solving the problem for him or her.

Spirit Whisperers do not take on a student's problem. Their efforts are directed toward returning the problem to where it rightfully belongs, squarely on the back of the student involved.

Matt, a sixth-grader, attended an elementary school that held a formal graduation ceremony to honor the students who would be moving on to seventh grade. All three of the sixth-grade teachers informed students of the date and laid out the ground rules. Because the seating capacity in the all-purpose room was limited, each student was asked to invite only two guests to witness their rite of passage into seventh grade.

Matt immediately informed his parents of the situation. His mother responded affirmatively to his invitation. His father regretfully declined, as he had unchangeable, out-of-town work commitments on the date of the graduation.

One guest under the limit, Matt called to invite his sister, who was attending a state college. She was excited about being invited and told Matt, "I'd love to come. I'll be there for sure and I'll bring my boyfriend."

The unexpected announcement of a third person was a surprise to Matt and caught him off guard. Not knowing for sure how to handle this emerging situation, he chose to say nothing. The next day he presented his problem to his teacher.

When Matt informed his teacher of the recent developments with his sister, he did not say, "I have a problem." Nor were his words, "I'm struggling with a situation and I would like some help." He said instead, "*We* have a problem," carefully inserting his teacher into the equation with his language.

The efficient way to handle this problem would be to tell Matt what to do. "You'll just have to call your sister and explain the situation to her," his teacher could have said. "Tell her you're sorry, but there just isn't room to have her boyfriend attend."

Efficient? Yes. Effective? Probably not. Not if your goal is to help students learn to own and solve their own problems. Not if you want to discourage students from coming to you for solutions in the future. Not if your desire is to implement the Principle of Personal Responsibility.

Spirit Whisperers don't equate "efficient" with "effective." They realize that good teaching is not always time-efficient— that teaching to a child's spirit often takes an investment of time up front to help them learn how to do things for themselves. Short-term, it's more efficient to tie a child's shoe than to teach him to do it himself. It's quicker to find an appropriate book for a student than to teach her how she can find one for herself. It takes less time to solve students' problems than to teach them to solve problems on their own.

Spirit Whisperers don't concern themselves with being efficient. Their goal is to be effective.

"Sounds like you have a problem. That's a bummer," Matt's teacher responded when she heard his description of the situation. With those words she kept the responsibility for the problem where it belonged—with Matt. Through her choice of language she also launched a series of teacher skills designed to resist the temptation to rescue, thus helping Matt to see himself as capable. She began to implement the Problem-Return Technique.

The Problem-Return Technique, also taught in Performance Learning Systems classes, allows Spirit Whisperers to help without taking over for the student, to communicate empathy early in the process, and to help the student learn how to solve problems. The technique helps Spirit Whisperers stay clear of the rescuer role and allows them to offer support, encouragement, and ideas without over-functioning.

The Problem-Return Technique consists of seven steps.

1. SEND EMPATHY AND OWNERSHIP STATEMENTS.
2. ASK FOR POSSIBLE SOLUTIONS.
3. GET PERMISSION TO OFFER SUGGESTIONS.
4. GIVE SUGGESTIONS.
5. SEND A RESPONSE-ABILITY STATEMENT.
6. DELIVER A SHORT POWER/VICTIM LECTURE BURST.
7. EXIT.

The following comments from students reveal an attempt to give their problem to an adult. Each signals an appropriate time to put the Problem-Return Technique to use.

- "I forgot my lunch (homework, permission slip, band instrument, gym shoes, picture money, white shirt for the concert, etc.)."
- "My dad didn't sign the slip."
- "I hate my group. I never get to say anything."
- "I never get to be captain in physical education."
- "No one wants to play with me."
- "I can't find my notebook."
- "I had the report done, but I lost it."

- "I can't get the book back to you in time because my report isn't finished."
- "I don't know what to do for my science fair project."

Matt's teacher recognized his attempt to eliminate his problem by assigning it to her. Refusing to accept it, she gave it back to him with, "Sounds like you have a problem. That's a bummer." With those words, she skillfully completed the first step of the Problem-Return Technique, the delivery of Empathy and Ownership Statements.

"That's a bummer" conveys empathy. Other possibilities Matt's teacher could have used include, "That's too bad," "What a shame," "I'm sorry to hear that." Empathetic Teacher Talk sends the implied message, "I care. I'm concerned. I feel for you."

"Sounds like you have a problem" indicates ownership. It points to the person who really has the problem. Other words that convey problem ownership and give the problem back to the student include:

- "That's an interesting problem you have there."
- "That's a tough situation you've created."
- "You're faced with an exciting opportunity here."
- "Sounds like you've created some real drama in your life."
- "You've put yourself behind the eight-ball on this one, eh?"
- "Seems like you're in pretty deep."

At first glance, you might think a Spirit Whisperer sends an Ownership Statement so the student hears that this is his problem. While that's a valuable and appreciated outcome, it's not the main reason for delivering an Ownership Statement. A Spirit Whisperer's number one reason for saying, "Sounds like you have a problem," is so they, themselves, hear it. It serves as a reminder to them that this is not *their* problem. They use it as a warning to themselves. It signals that danger is ahead—the danger of possibly taking over and rescuing a student.

As soon as Matt's teacher reminded herself and Matt that this was *his* problem, she went on to step two in the Problem-Return Technique. She asked for possible solutions. "What ideas do you have for solving this?" she asked. Matt's response was predictable. "I don't know," he replied.

Spirit Whisperers don't ask for possible solutions because they think the student is going to reel off four possibilities they've been considering and then announce their favorite. They know that more often than not the student is going to come back with "Beats me" or "Darned if I know." Still, Spirit Whisperers ask, "What choices do you see here?," "How do you think you'll handle this?," or "What options are available to you?" They ask this type of question because the implied message is "I see you as capable. I see you as a problem solver." Adults only extend that kind of invitation to people they see as competent. Spirit Whisperers want the student to know that he or she is seen as a competent solution seeker.

After Matt's "I don't know" response, his teacher moved to step three and issued an invitation to suggest alternatives. "Would you like to hear some possibilities that other sixth-graders have used in the past to solve this kind of problem?" she asked. "I guess so" was his response.

Notice that Matt's teacher couched her question in terms of students his age. That raises the odds that you'll get a favorable response. If you ask, "Do you want to hear some of *my* ideas," you're likely to get a "no" reaction. "Want to hear some things I've seen other seniors do when they lose their note cards?" or "I've seen many fourth-graders forget their lunch over the years. Would you like to hear how some of them solved that problem?" are examples of framing the question in an age-sensitive manner.

Suggesting alternatives without first getting the student's permission is inappropriate. Spirit Whisperers let students decide if they are receptive to suggestions. If the student chooses not to continue the process, the teacher respects that choice and allows the student space and time to struggle on alone.

Having received an affirmative response from Matt, his teacher continued, "I'll suggest a few things I've seen other sixth-graders do with a similar problem. If you think of any possibilities as we go along, add them to the list." Her list included:

1. TALK YOUR MOTHER INTO NOT COMING.
2. CALL YOUR SISTER AND EXPLAIN.
3. WRITE YOUR SISTER A LETTER.
4. HAVE A PARTY AFTERWARDS AND INVITE MORE PEOPLE.
5. SEND YOUR SISTER AN E-MAIL CARD ALONG WITH AN APOLOGY.
6. SEE IF YOU CAN FIND A FRIEND WHO IS ONLY HAVING ONE GUEST AND ASK IF YOU CAN USE THAT SPACE FOR YOUR SISTER'S BOYFRIEND.

With the list of possible alternatives complete, Matt's teacher moved on to the next step of the Problem-Return Technique and delivered a Response-Ability Statement. "One of the things I've learned about you this year, Matt, is that once you see choices, you're always able to come up with one that works for you," she told him.

A Response-Ability Statement affirms a student's strengths. It communicates your belief in the student's ability to solve his problem. The implied message is, "I see you as capable and response-able."

Immediately following the Response-Ability Statement is the brief Power/Victim Lecture Burst. The Power/Victim Lecture Burst is the portion of this process where you inform students they can choose to solve or not solve their problem. It is where you hand the problem back to the student for a decision on how to handle it. It is, once again, where you honor the boundary of allowing students to own the problem. It is where they get to come face-to-face with the Principle of Personal Responsibility.

Matt listened as his teacher reviewed his options. "Matt, we have two kinds of kids at this school. There are those who choose to be powerful and those who choose to be a victim. You have a choice now. You can choose to take the power stance or choose to act as a victim.

"Students who choose the power stance look over the alternatives for solving their problem and pick one they think might work for them. They put it into effect and see what happens. Many times it works and they get to feel successful. Sometimes it doesn't work. If it doesn't, they often try a second solution. Even if every effort at solving their problem is unsuccessful, they still feel somewhat power-full because they didn't just accept the situation without attempting to do something about it. They made an effort to solve it, and that feels good to most people.

"The other choice you have is to play victim. Victims say to themselves, 'There's nothing I can do,' 'It won't work anyway,' or 'Poor me.' They choose to do nothing, or they go unconscious and forget about it. They do get something, though. They get to feel sorry for themselves. They get to feel miserable and without power. They get to run around telling everyone how awful and unfair their life is.

"Guess who gets to decide in this classroom whether to be a victim or a power person? That's right—the students. And guess who gets to decide in this case? That's right—you do. I'm looking forward to hearing how you choose to handle this one. I think you're up to it."

After successfully handing the problem back to her student, Matt's teacher made her exit. Notice that she didn't say, "And I know you'll make a good choice," or "I'm sure you'll make the right choice." *All* choices are seen as the right choice. If Matt picks an alternative and it works for him, that's a good choice. If he decides to do the victim stance and gets valuable feedback on what that feels like and stays conscious of the results he produces, then that's the right choice for him at this time. Either choice can be a valuable learning experience.

Spirit Whisperers believe they do more for their students by doing less. Teachers who tell their students what to do and what not to do are betraying the Principle of Personal Responsibility by taking responsibility away from them. Clear boundaries dictate that you are responsible for you. Your students are responsible for themselves. Anything less is an invasion of space and a trespass on personal responsibility. We serve our students best when we help them get in touch with their total responsibility in a situation.

Likewise, we serve ourselves best when we get in touch with *our* total responsibility in a situation. Responsibility means not blaming anything or anyone else for our present situation. If we can blame our students, principal, spouse, curriculum, Board of Education, union, secretary, computer, textbook, superintendent, or our students' parents, we don't have to take responsibility for the results or lack of results we create.

Responsibility also means not blaming ourselves. We need to eliminate the words "blame" and "fault" from our vocabulary. Think of "fault" as an f-word. Think of "blame" as an f-word, also. Blame and fault are not the issue. It's all a matter of choice.

Choice relates to cause. We, like our students, get to be cause in our life, based on the choices we make.

Responsibility is ours if we choose to take it. We are responsible for what we choose and what we believe. We are responsible for what we think and what we see. We are responsible for what we choose to do and how we decide to be. We are responsible for the level of personal power we retain and for how much we give away.

As Spirit Whisperers, we are also responsible for teaching and demonstrating the Principle of Personal Power, the subject of the next chapter.

CHAPTER 5

The Principle of Personal Power

L abor problems accompanied the opening of school at a large city school district in Michigan recently. The teachers, unsatisfied with the lack of progress with contract negotiations, voted to begin the school year without a new contract. As part of their vote to start the school year on time, the teachers decided to demonstrate their dissatisfaction to the Board of Education and show their solidarity by performing only those duties that were legally required by the current contract. They would fulfill their regular teaching responsibilities and behave as professionals in the classroom, while refusing to volunteer for any extra assignments.

Consequently, no one was available to lead the debate team. No volunteer organized the foreign language, physics, National Honor Society, or varsity clubs. Teachers declined opportunities to run the concession stands and take tickets at athletic events. No safety patrol sponsor could be found among the teaching ranks. The powder puff football game between senior and junior girls was canceled for lack of adult supervision. Administrators were left alone to monitor halls, lunch-rooms, and the loading and unloading of buses.

As the contract negotiations dragged on, the process became increasingly public. Each day teacher leaders, Board of Education members, and parents were quoted in the local newspaper concerning the situation. The teachers' union placed full-page ads in the newspaper. The Board of Education sent letters to all parents. A special Board meeting was held so parents could voice their concerns and frustrations.

Back at school it was business as usual. The teachers taught professionally. Math, history, literature, music, art, business, and technology concepts were presented, reviewed, and tested.

No mention was made of the labor dispute from the front of the classroom. If students asked about it, teachers politely informed them that the classroom was for study of biology or creative writing. The subject matter lessons continued. So did the contract dispute.

The Board of Education members, teachers, parents, and elected city officials all had a voice in this conflict. Each found outlets for expressing his or her position and concerns. Engaged in an emotional power struggle, they wrestled back and forth, flexing their muscles, groping for advantage, attempting to position themselves in the best possible light to influence public opinion.

As the dispute wore on, students grew increasingly restless with the undercurrent of dissatisfaction in which their school was marinating. They missed the extracurricular activities to which they had been accustomed. They felt lost in the process, voiceless, and unempowered.

In an attempt to demonstrate their dissatisfaction and inform the adults that they too were growing frustrated, several students organized a 20-minute walkout. They decided that on October 4, at 10 minutes past 10 o'clock, those students who chose to participate would get up, walk out of class, and proceed to the front of the building. There they would sit in the grass for 20 minutes. When the fourth hour bell rang, the plan was to return to class and go on with their school day. The students' silent, non-violent protest would be their way of saying, "No one is listening to us. We have some concerns here. Please stop and take notice. Please listen. We are being affected and we don't like what is happening."

The administration discovered the students' plan two hours before its activation and hurriedly sprang into action. A conference among the principal, the assistant principal, and the two school counselors, along with a phone call to the superintendent, brought action.

Ten minutes prior to the intended walkout, the principal used the public address system to make an announcement. "This is your principal speaking," he said. "We are aware of the plan some of you have to walk out of school in the middle of third hour to protest the state of contract negotiations. I want you to know we have photographers poised at each exit. We will photograph each student who leaves the building. Each student identified leaving the building will be suspended for three days and will not be re-admitted until we hold a suspension hearing with you and your parents. Let me repeat this so there is no misunderstanding. This is your principal speaking. We are aware . . ."

No student left the building that day.

It is difficult to imagine what was learned related to algebra, French, American history, or other subject areas in the remaining hours of that school day. It is not difficult to imagine what was learned in relation to the Principle of Personal Power.

Students learned that adults give orders; students obey. Adults make decisions; students follow them. Adults have power; students do not. Many students learned that adults fear giving them a legitimate voice in their own school lives.

Imagine if this situation had been handled in a school staffed by Spirit Whisperers.

Upon hearing of the students' plan to walk out third hour, the principal, assistant principal, and the two counselors immediately convene. An hour later they personally distribute an important written communiqué to each teacher. It states:

> It has come to our attention that some students intend to walk out of class third hour and sit in front of the building to protest the state of contract negotiations. Do not be surprised if several of your students join in this demonstration. Continue to teach your class as usual with those students who choose to remain. Make a list of those who decide to leave, as we will need to mark them absent from your class for that period. This absence should be treated as any other regularly occurring absence during the semester.
>
> We see this situation as an opportunity to help students learn about the concept of peaceful demonstration and the role it has played in our country's history. Also, this is a chance for us to help students face and deal with the important issues of peer pressure, consequences, and decision-making.
>
> When students return, use your next full class period to debrief the situation with them. Have them respond to the questions which we have provided below or similar questions of your

choice. A class discussion to help your students appreciate the divergent perspectives they hold would be a helpful way to end the hour.

1.   HOW DID YOU DECIDE WHETHER TO STAY OR LEAVE?

2.   WHAT DID YOU GET AND WHAT DID YOU HAVE TO GIVE UP BECAUSE OF THE CHOICE YOU MADE IN REGARD TO STAYING IN CLASS OR WALKING OUT?

3.   WHAT EVENTS IN HISTORY ARE SIMILAR TO WHAT YOU EXPERIENCED HERE AT THIS SCHOOL TODAY?

4.   WHAT GENERALIZATIONS CAN YOU MAKE ABOUT THIS TYPE OF PROTEST?

5.   WHAT DO YOU THINK WAS THE GOAL OF THOSE WHO WALKED OUT AND DO YOU FEEL THEY ACCOMPLISHED THEIR OBJECTIVE?

In addition to discussing these issues in class, you could have students write up their reactions to the event as a homework assignment and turn it in tomorrow.

Our goal here is to help students examine this event and the role they played in it by thinking and writing about it. We see this as an important opportunity to help students get in touch with their personal power.

Thank you for your cooperation.

Implementing the Principle of Personal Power is not without risk. Sure, students could leave the school grounds and move into the business district. Yes, students could linger on the school lawn for more than one class period. It is possible that the local newspaper could print photographs and an article critical of the school officials. Yes, someone could even get hurt.

Squelching the pending demonstration is also not without risk. Resentment of the power play by school officials could result in vandalism to the school grounds. Students could organize a sick-out and miss an entire day or more of school. Students' sense of personal power, enthusiasm, and motivation could be deadened. Student hopelessness could be the primary result. Yes, someone could get hurt.

The key word in the Principle of Personal Power is "power." This does not mean power over. It does not mean power to force or coerce. The type of power under consideration here is an inner sense of personal power. The word "power" comes from the Latin word *potere*, which means "to be able." A Spirit Whisperer's goal is to empower students by helping them see themselves as able, capable, valuable, and response-able.

In each of the scenarios above, did the educators' response help the students see themselves as more capable or less capable? Did it expand their sense of personal power or diminish it? Did it help them to believe in themselves or did it encourage doubt? Did it assist them in gaining a sense of unlimited potential or did it help them perceive themselves as confined?

A goal of Spirit Whisperers in attempting to implement the Principle of Personal Power is the creation of "power with" rather than "power over." "Power with" shares control. It helps students to develop inner control and, as quickly as possible, to shed their need for control from without.

Much of what you have already read in the previous chapters has been an effort to empower students. Getting them in touch with the creative force of their thoughts, words, and deeds is one such attempt. So are teaching the concepts of attribute awareness and the effort to help students appreciate the cause-and-effect relationship that exists within the choices they make. Teaching self-responsible language, helping students make a "be" choice, and allowing opportunities for self-evaluation are more ways in which Spirit Whisperers empower students.

In addition to the empowering strategies already presented, Spirit Whisperers are invested in helping students take ever-increasing amounts of control over their school lives. To that end, Spirit Whisperers work to make themselves dispensable. They enjoy feeling unneeded. They know their greatest gift to their students is to empower them so that they become independent as well as interdependent.

Everything you do as a teacher to make yourself dispensable makes your students more independent. And everything you do that makes you indispensable in the classroom makes your students more dependent—upon you. Where are you on this issue? Are you teaching your students to get along without you or to need you?

Shared Control

One way in which Spirit Whisperers make themselves dispensable and implement the Principle of Personal Power is to share control with students. Shared control is a style of classroom management that helps students experience freedom and security simultaneously. It provides the basic structure and allows students to make decisions and exercise control within the perimeter of that structure.

"I'm not going to share control with students," a teacher informed me at one of my full-day seminars. "They can't handle it. They're not responsible enough. What if someone gets hurt? I need to be in control. I'm paid to have control and I'd get fired if I didn't keep control of my classroom. I'm not sharing control with students who don't know how to control themselves."

Don't misinterpret here. Spirit Whisperers are very much in control of their classrooms. They wouldn't want it any other way. Shared control is a classroom management strategy for teachers who *want* control; it is not a way of *giving up* control. In fact, with a shared control style, teachers often end up with more control than if they had attempted to take total control.

"How can that be?" you might wonder. If you have some control, and share part of what you have, how could you possibly end up with more? How can you have more if you give away some of what you have?

In a shared control classroom, students have some say, but not the final say, in how things operate. They help set the rules and create the limits, and they have input on solving problems that occur. Above all, they are heard. They have a voice in decisions affecting them. And because they participate actively in the construction of the environment, they feel some ownership in its creation. They experience their personal power and come to realize they can influence their own school lives. As a result of being part of a shared control classroom, they are less likely to activate the new "three R's"—resistance, reluctance, and resentment. They are less likely to cause discipline problems. They are more likely to choose self-control.

If you alone determine the rules, it then becomes your role to enforce those rules and it becomes the students' role to resist. You can invest much time playing police person in that way. If you and the class decide together on ways of operating and on solutions to problems that occur, you will find more people ready to help enforce the rules that were mutually agreed upon. Although it seems paradoxical, because they are willing to create more controllers Spirit Whisperers actually end up with more control in their classrooms.

Offering controlled choice is one way in which Spirit Whisperers share control and activate the Principle of Personal Power in their classrooms. There is power in choice, for both teachers and students. Power is shared when teachers use controlled choice by setting specific limits that allow choice within those limits. Teachers have power and control because they determine the choices and the limits. Students have power and control because they get to decide from among the alternatives.

Controlled choice is preferable to unlimited choice. Unlimited choice can be overwhelming to students, and they often have difficulty deciding what to do. I was once invited by a kindergarten teacher to do an observation of what she termed "Choice Time." She wanted me to help her figure out why chaos reigned during that time period and why her six-year-olds were having such difficulty making choices and sticking with them.

I didn't watch Choice Time for long before my observations matched her perception. Chaos was indeed an accurate descriptor of that portion of her day.

"What choices do the students have during Choice Time?" I asked during our after school conference.

"Students can do whatever they want," she informed me. "It's Choice Time. They can choose to get down any of the puzzles, use the dress-up clothes in the closet, or play with the blocks in the building center. They can choose from any of the toys or games on the shelf or use any of a variety of materials at the art center. The sand and water area is also available. There are three shelves of books they can look at, and the paint area is open at that time as well."

Choice Time was chaotic because there were simply too many choices. I suggested to this teacher that she limit the choices by putting out four puzzles, five books, and a limited number of materials at the art center. My recommendations included having available only a portion of the dress-up clothes, games, and toys.

The results were predictable. The youngsters relaxed into the structure and were more able to effectively choose from a limited menu than they were from the open-ended number of choices. Chaos was eliminated as the students learned to make choices from within the structure.

Examples of other controlled choices follow:

- "You can do your final draft on red or green paper. You choose."
- "Here are three famous Americans. Choose one on whom to do your report."
- "All of you have to make a demonstration speech. It must follow the guidelines as indicated on the paper I am distributing. You can decide what skill you want to demonstrate."
- "You can decide which Midwest state to use for your report. Your report must cover the following . . ."
- "You can choose one piece of poster board or three sheets of construction paper."
- "On page 47, you can do the odds or the evens to demonstrate your understanding of fractions."
- "You can use any three crayons from the crayon box to create your poster."
- "Here are three important events in Martin Luther King's life. Choose one for your writing topic."

Limited choice is an example of shared control in action. You control the number of choices and their boundaries. The student controls the decisions to be made within those boundaries. Both parties are at choice. Both have some degree of control. Both get to experience the Principle of Personal Power at work in their lives.

Your students' ability to make choices begins with your decisions of how, when, and if to offer them. You can elect to present students with controlled choices or not. You can share control or keep it all for yourself. It's your choice.

INVITING STUDENT INPUT

Another way in which Spirit Whisperers share control in their classrooms is by inviting student input. These teachers actively seek student opinions, ideas, suggestions, and concerns on a wide variety of topics.

SHARING TIME

A sixth-grade teacher implemented a regularly scheduled sharing time for her students. During that weekly process, students were invited to share their ideas, thoughts, and feelings. The teacher controlled the topic, announcing it in advance, and kept the discussion on target. Topics included: sharing what you liked about your art project; your opinion of the hot lunch program; telling about a hobby; expectations or concerns about moving on to the middle school; ideas on how to improve the state of the world today; a paragraph from a favorite book; a meaningful quote and a two-sentence explanation of what the quote means to you.

JOURNAL WRITING

Many Spirit Whisperers also use journal writing to invite student input. Again, teachers frequently choose to structure the topic. Occasionally, journal writing is non-structured. Topics may include:

- I'd like your opinion on what happened on the playground today. How did you see it? What did that disturbance look like from your point of view?
- I'm going to be rearranging the classroom next week. I'd like your ideas on how to do that. Please offer some suggestions and give me reasons for those suggestions.
- We're going to be choosing a class name. List as many suggestions as you can and tell me about the one you like best.
- This is Respect Week at school. Why do you suppose respect was chosen? What type of respect would you like to receive from classmates?
- What was your favorite learning activity this week? Explain.
- React to the assembly we had today and tell me what you thought of it.

Teachers who use journals respect students' right to privacy. If a student does not want to share a particular entry with the teacher, he folds that page back and paperclips it shut. That's the agreed upon signal that the page is private. Spirit Whisperers respect that signal.

All other journal entries are read by the teacher and responded to in writing. Spirit Whisperers focus on the content and react to students' ideas and concerns, often asking further questions. Mechanics of writing are ignored or noted for use in designing content lessons later. Journal entries are not the place to correct spelling and punctuation errors. There are times in the day when Spirit Whisperers work hard on those skills. Journal time is not one of them.

PARAGRAPH PILES

A high school teacher uses file cards to create what he calls "Paragraph Piles." Once a week he designs an opinion-seeking question and allows students five minutes to write a paragraph on the file card, stating their opinions. He collects the completed cards and puts them in a pile on his desk. Two students then split the piles and alternately read the opinions expressed on the cards. No names are attached. A class discussion follows. Emphasis is on hearing and understanding the different opinions. There are no right or wrong answers. Not all opinions are agreed with. Every opinion is respected.

Sharing control by inviting student opinion could be as simple as constructing "I urge . . ." telegrams or an add-on opinion chain. In classes using "I urge . . ." telegrams, students select a real person and design a pretend telegram to urge them to take a particular stance or choose a specific action. Add-on opinion chains work by having class members write an opinion about a common topic on a strip of paper. The strips are then linked together to make a paper chain.

CLASS MEETINGS

A more thorough seeking of student input occurs when teachers hold regularly scheduled class meetings to plan events, address concerns, or search for solutions. Jason Roberts did just that following several incidents of pushing and shoving near the drinking fountain in his classroom. The horseplay occurred as his students were coming in from recess. On hot days, the fifth-graders hurried to get in line for drinks. Since many of them wanted to be first, or near the front of the line, a scrambling, lunging scene ensued that held the possibility of serious injury. Jason had visions of teeth lying in the sink while he made a phone call to parents informing them of their child's need for emergency dental surgery. He knew it was time for a class meeting and time to involve students in the search for solutions.

Jason did not view this situation as a problem. He saw it as an opportunity to lead his students through a solution-seeking process while implementing the Principle of Personal Power.

Keep in mind that Jason needed no student input to find a solution that would eliminate the pushing and shoving. All he had to do was assert his authority and announce, "No more recess for three days for anyone who pushes or shoves around the drinking fountain." Enforce that teacher-created solution a few times and the unsafe situation disappears. Quick and efficient.

Jason, however, is not one of those educators who equate "efficient" with "effective." As a Spirit Whisperer, he realizes that efficient and effective are not synonymous. He resisted "doing power" to students and opted instead to gather them together and lead them through a solution-seeking process.

This fifth-grade teacher began the solution-seeking class meeting by sharing his perceptions. He informed students about what he had observed over the past several days. He used descriptive Teacher Talk, telling them only what he had seen and heard. His remarks were void of evaluation. His comments did include information that spelled out the potential danger of pushing and shoving around the drinking fountain.

"I've noticed that some of you run into the room and hurry to the drinking fountain," Jason said. "Whoever gets there first begins to drink and others come piling up behind. Bumping and shoving occur as you attempt to get a spot near the front of the line. I've seen incidents where the person drinking gets shoved from behind. There is potential for serious injury here, and I'm concerned for your safety."

When he was done sharing his observations, Jason shifted gears and moved into the listening mode. "That's how I perceive the situation," he said, beginning his transition from speaking to listening. "Now please share with me your perceptions. What does that drinking fountain scene look like and feel like to you? Help me appreciate it from your perspective."

He got a variety of responses.

- "It's hot out and we're thirsty."
- "It's fun."
- "We like to see who can be first."
- "We don't have enough time to get drinks."
- "Some people hog the drinking fountain."
- "I got pushed out of the way once and almost got knocked down."
- "I agree it's dangerous."
- "Some people are so rude, I don't even feel like getting a drink."

"It certainly sounds like we have the need for a solution here," Jason concluded. "Let's see if we can come up with a short statement of our need, and I'll write it on the board so we can all see. That way we can focus on it when we look for solutions, and it will help us stay on track."

Following several revisions, a statement of need emerged. It read, *We need a safe procedure for getting drinks after recess.*

After writing the statement of need on the chalkboard, Jason then led his fifth-graders through a brainstorming session in which they suggested possible solutions. Ideas were listed as they were spoken. No effort was made to evaluate or discuss them. No names were attached to the suggestions. The process continued until the idea producers had exhausted their supply of alternatives.

With the list in full view of the entire class, Jason moved the process along by stating, "Let's talk about which ideas you think will work for us. Remember, our goal is to come up with a solution that will create a safe procedure for getting drinks after recess."

Students then discussed the ideas they felt were most workable. The less practical ideas were not berated; they were simply not discussed.

In the course of the discussion, two ideas were blended into one, resulting in the solution that made consensus possible. Students decided that they could run in from recess up to the hall door. Once they reached that door, they would walk down the hall, into the classroom, and over to the drinking fountain.

When it appeared that the synergistically created solution had the backing of many students, Jason took the class outside for a trial run. The students role-played their suggestion twice during the field test and confirmed their beliefs that their proposed solution would make the drinking fountain situation safer.

Upon re-entering the classroom, Jason made the following proposal: "How about putting this solution into effect for one week to see how it works? Thumbs up if you'd be willing to go along with this idea."

Every student flashed thumbs. The symbolic thumbs-up gesture was an act of closure that meant everyone agreed or was willing to go along for the good of the group.

Jason then wrote the solution on the board along with a date one week from the time of that meeting. Students knew from previous class meetings that they would be meeting again to report on whether and how the solution was working. If their efforts didn't produce a safer scene around the drinking fountain after recess, they knew they would be back in the solution-seeking process, searching for an alternative that would work.

Jason Roberts invested forty-five minutes to lead students through this process. Forty-five minutes not spent on teaching reading, long division, or spelling. Forty-five minutes not spent studying for tests, creating art, or learning the parts of speech. Was it worth it?

His investment of forty-five minutes helped Jason's students perceive themselves as part of the solution rather than part of a problem. It helped them experience group cohesiveness, see themselves as part of a larger whole, and build a sense of belonging. It allowed students and teacher to be on the same side, working together in search of solutions. They experienced no one as the enemy. The problem wasn't even seen as a problem, but rather as an opportunity.

In forty-five minutes students learned that taking ownership for a situation means taking responsibility for finding solutions. They learned to trust their own solution-seeking abilities and rely on themselves and on one another. They experienced the self-responsible behaviors of making a plan and following through. They got in touch with their own power.

Was it worth it? Spirit Whisperers don't even ask that question. They already know the answer.

Another method Spirit Whisperers use to implement the Principle of Personal Power is to focus on the teaching of skills. They know that students who possess skills have more response-ability and a greater sense of personal power than students who lack skills have.

If you're a skilled typist, you have a greater chance of achieving success than someone without typing skills has. If you can speak fluently in two languages, you're more empowered than is a person who knows only one language. If you don't possess reading skills, you're at a disadvantage when compared to those who can read. There is a certain degree of power than comes with being able to write and speak effectively—power that you don't have if you lack those skills. The equation is simple: *increased skills equals increased personal power*.

Spirit Whisperers teach content skills with a passion. They teach students how to serve a volleyball, how to use the lathe safely and accurately, how to subtract, and how to construct a complete sentence. They help students learn the skills of dividing fractions, making contractions, following the scientific method, completing a neck-spring, playing the flute, and surfing the Internet. They teach spelling and help students expand their vocabulary.

But while Spirit Whisperers value their role of helping students master content skills, they extend their teaching of skills into other, equally important, areas. They teach the skills of ignoring distractions, setting attainable goals, and budgeting time; of organizing tasks and materials, managing anger, picturing positively, and eliminating self-interference. They teach study skills, interpersonal skills, and social skills.

As outlined in earlier chapters, Spirit Whisperers teach the skills of self-evaluation, checking it out inside, making a "be" choice, managing thoughts, and choosing perceptions. They teach self-responsible language and how to search for solutions. These skills, like content skills, empower students and increase their response-ability.

MIND SKILLS

Mind skills are a special category of skill training highly valued by Spirit Whisperers. We teach students to manage time, materials, the environment, and their bodies. Why not help them manage the biocomputer that sits on their shoulders—their minds? Many people spend more time intentionally managing the hair that sits on the top of their head than they spend managing what goes on inside that head.

As the popular slogan informs us, "A mind is a terrible thing to waste." The state of our mind determines our perceptions of the events and circumstances that occur in our lives. The responses we make to those events depend on how we perceive them, so our minds affect everything that happens to us. What occurs in our mind is too important to leave to chance. Therefore, Spirit Whisperers regularly practice and teach mind skills.

Mind skills, taught in Successful Teaching for Acceptance of Responsibility™, a course I designed for Performance Learning Systems, are a series of skills intended to help students get in touch with the power they have over how they perceive, feel, think, and act. Once learned, mind skills are ways to re-mind yourself so you can consciously influence the events of your life and produce the results you desire.

LOOKING FOR THE DOUGHNUT

One mind skill Spirit Whisperers teach and use themselves is called Looking for the Doughnut. Learning to use your mind to "look for the doughnut" is about purposefully looking for what *is* there in the situation before you, rather than looking for what is *not* there.

Many people spend their lives looking for the hole rather than for the doughnut. Guess what they usually find? That's right, holes. If you look for holes, you find them. If you look for pieces of the doughnut, you find them as well.

If you are using this mind skill as you read this book, you are actively looking for strategies that you can immediately put to work in your classroom. And you are doing so with intentionality. Since people generally find what they're looking for, ideas are surfacing for you, flowing from these pages as well as from your own creative mind.

If you're looking for holes, you will find those as well. You will notice that some paragraphs are better written than others are. You will see that I tend to overuse some words. Your perception may be that there are sections in this book that are not as detailed as you would like. Perhaps you will find passages where I ramble on far too long for your taste, or where I repeat myself.

The point is this: you can make a conscious choice to look for the doughnut or to look for the hole. Whatever choice you make will affect what you see. And what you see is what you get. To change what you get, change what you look for. Re-mind yourself to look for the doughnut. Then create ways to teach this mind skill to your students.

BOOMERANG STATEMENTS

A second mind skill is the use of Boomerang Statements. Boomerang Statements are verbal responses that students can use to turn around the negative energy sent their way through put-downs, criticism, sarcasm, or accusation, transforming it into positive energy.

A Boomerang Statement is a positive response to a verbal attack. It is used to re-mind yourself that what *you* think or believe is more important than the taunt or put-down you just received. It helps the student not to take offense and to send a communication back to the sender that is free of negative energy. The skill enables the student to neither take offense nor send it.

If the initial statement is "Girls can't throw very well," the Boomerang Statement could be "Girls can throw just fine" or "There is a woman's softball team that competes in the Olympics." A comment such as "You made a stupid mistake" can be turned around with "I learn from every mistake I make" or "Mistakes are necessary for learning."

A student who can effectively send positive Boomerang Statements in the face of shaming or taunting is more responseable than one who cannot. Spirit Whisperers help students become skilled at making that type of response.

TURN THE PAGE

Turn the Page is another mind skill that helps students tune into their own power and use it effectively in their lives. Turn the Page is a symbolic demonstration that re-minds students that the past is over and the present is where their power lies.

"As you know from yesterday, we didn't do well as a class on our first Spanish test," Mrs. Gliess informed her fourth-hour students. "Most of you were disappointed. I was disappointed. And some of your parents were probably disappointed. Yesterday we spent the entire hour going over the answers and examining your responses in detail. Many of you learned where and perhaps why you didn't do as well as you desired.

"Today we're going to do something a little bit different," she continued. "Please take out your journals and turn to the next clean page. Put your test score in the middle of the page and circle it. When I give the signal, I want you to use that same page and write for five minutes. Write about your feelings concerning your grade, what you learned, what you attribute your grade to, what you could have done differently. Fill the page. Write in words, phrases, or complete sentences. Throw in some Spanish if you choose. "Okay, *puden empesen*. Begin."

Mrs. Gliess called time exactly five minutes later. "Now," she said, "take hold of the upper right-hand corner of the page. Everybody got it? Together, on the count of three, I want you to turn the page. Ready? *Uno, dos, tres* . . .

"What do you see?" she asked, after everyone had done as instructed. Her students, unsure of what the right answer might be, responded with only blank stares.

"What do you see?" she asked again.

"A blank page," someone finally said.

"Nothing" and "An empty piece of paper" were the tentative responses offered by two other students.

"Exactly," the teacher said. "There is nothing there. You have an empty page, a clean slate. You have just turned the page on your first Spanish test of the semester. Think of turning the page as leaving the past behind. There is nothing any of you can do about what happened yesterday. It's over. It's not even a dot on the horizon.

"Of course, learn whatever lessons you need to learn from that test. But then turn the page mentally, the way we just did physically. Your only point of power is now. Turning the page is a symbolic gesture that you can take at any time to re-mind yourself that from this moment on you are starting anew, with a clean slate.

"It's time for us to move forward now. Please turn to page 37 in your texts and let's begin again."

When students have internalized the mind skill of turning the page, they can put it to use in their lives in a variety of situations. When they get cut from the team, get turned down for a date, get passed over for the role they wanted in the play, or simply have a bad day, they can turn the page in their minds. Whether they actually write the incident on a page and turn it or turn the page in their imagination is immaterial. What matters most is that students develop the power to create a clean slate whenever they need one using the mind skill of Turn the Page.

Put Turn the Page to work in your own life. Still upset about a remark made by a colleague? Turn the page. Get turned down for the chairmanship of an important committee? Turn the page. Have a frustrating day with your principal? Turn the page. Sick of this section of this book? Turn the page.

SHAKE IT OFF

Shake It Off is another mind skill taught by Spirit Whisperers. A high school teacher noticed several students nodding off as he showed a video on drug education. Not wanting these students to miss the important content contained in the video, he shut off the television and turned on the classroom lights.

"Everyone please stand up," he announced to his surprised class. "I see that some of you are tired and are having trouble staying awake. Me, too. Let's do what I do when I drive long distances and I'm feeling tired. I stop the car, get out, and shake it off."

He then demonstrated by shaking all over, moving every part of his body. Students acted embarrassed but followed his model and shook off their tiredness. Upon conclusion of the 45-second activity, the students sat down and viewed the remainder of the movie. No one fell asleep.

Do your first-grade students get in a giggling mood? Have them stand up and shake off the sillies. Have your eighth-graders shake off their nervousness before their demonstration speech. Your basketball team can shake off the jitters in the locker room before they head to the court.

Have your class write frustrations on sticky notes and affix them to their hands. Then have them stand and shake their hands vigorously until they literally shake off their frustrations.

Let students know that Shake It Off can be done mentally as well as physically. Stuck on an algebra problem? Shake it off in your mind and move on. Get thrown out on a close play at first base? Shake it off in your head as you return to the dugout. Worried about how you'll do on the test? Use this mind skill and internally shake it off before you begin.

SUMMON A SAYING

Summon a Saying is yet another mind skill taught by Spirit Whisperers. These phrases, short enough to fit on a bumper sticker (does that make it an auto-suggestion?) can add confidence, encouragement, and personal power to your life. Examples include:

- Do it now.
- Go for it.
- Take a full cut.
- My point of power is now.
- Being right doesn't work.
- Stick with it.
- Shift happens.
- I don't settle.
- I'm enough.
- Be the one.

- What would love do now?
- Don't push the river.
- Live from the inside out.
- This, too, shall pass.
- I don't have to bite the hook.
- Act as if.
- Let applause in.
- Now is all there is.
- What is my next step?
- Mistakes are learning experiences.
- Be cause.
- Problems are an opportunity.

Summon a Saying is a way of contacting the coach within. It's a technique for dipping into your inner knowing and pulling out the exact encouraging phrase you need, just when you need it.

Have students design a bumper sticker for themselves that holds strong meaning. Encourage them to write it twenty times a day for one week. Repetitious writing will plant the phrase in their minds. Later, when they need it, the phrase will flash into their consciousness. When the phrase appears, it's time to act. Put the phrase into action if it feels appropriate.

QUOTATION STATION

Another mind skill along this same vein is the Quotation Station. Invest time collecting quotes with your students. Create a list of 50 to 100 quotes, depending on the age of your class. Have students read over the quote list and select their top 10. Invite them to reproduce their favorites in their class notebook, thus creating their own private Quotation Station. Encourage them to add to it whenever they find a meaningful quote. Here are some examples.

"Thinking about sanding a piece of wood doesn't do it."

"Starving man wait long time for roast duck to fly into mouth."
—Chinese proverb

*"Mistakes are always mistakes, or so I've heard them say . . . But
if it teaches a lesson, the mistake will go away."*
—Hucklebug

*"The more you do of what you've done, the more you'll get of
what you've got."*

*"Anytime you see a turtle on top of a fence post, you know he
had some help."*
—Alex Haley

"Try not. Do. Or do not. There is no try."
—Yoda, from *Star Wars*

"Life is like a jeweler's wheel. It can grind us down or polish us."

"If the horse you're riding dies, get off."

"In our differences we grow: in our sameness we connect."
—Virginia Satir

*"It may be too late already, but it is not as much too late
now as it will be later."*
—C. H. Weisart

*"Human beings can alter their lives by altering their
attitudes of mind."*
—William James

"Teachers open the door. You enter by yourself."
—Chinese Proverb

"If it's their drama, don't jump on the stage."

"You never have time. You create time."

The Quotation Station can be used to manage your own mind. The next time you commit an error in front of your class, remember Hucklebug. *"But if it teaches a lesson, the mistake will go away."* If you're tempted to rescue a student by doing for them what they could choose to do for themselves, think of the Chinese Proverb, *"Teachers open the door. Students enter by themselves."* Hold the door open wide and then stand back out of the way. The next time you contemplate offering students more of what is currently not working, recall *"If the horse dies, get off."*

HUM A TUNE

Hum a Tune is another mind skill designed to rearrange your mind to produce a desired result. Once again, you can use it in your own life as well as teach it to your students.

My favorite 10K race in Kalamazoo, Michigan includes what is known as Heartbreak Hill. This portion of the course, which occurs halfway into the race, is deceptive because as you reach what appears to be the summit of a steep incline, the remainder of the hill comes into view. Inaccurately named in my opinion, the hill doesn't break hearts as much as it has the potential to break spirits.

During my last running of the Kalamazoo Klassic, I began the race at a faster pace than I had intended. When I got to Heartbreak Hill I slowed down for the long and steady (I hoped) jog to the top. When I reached the first summit, my spirit and energy were drained. I decided, as many runners do, to walk to the top of the second incline. Just then I heard a band at the top of the hill playing the theme from the film *Rocky*.

Hey, if Rocky could do it, I could too! As I hummed along I continued to jog to the top and then on to the flatter, more runner-friendly portion of the course. I called on the theme from *Rocky* on several more occasions during the remainder of the race. And I finished (as did everyone who ran) as a winner.

Hum a Tune is a way to inspire yourself to keep going, to create quality, or to find peace and tranquility. "Born Free," the Lone Ranger's theme song, "Pacabel," "Row, Row, Row Your Boat," and "I'd Like to Teach the World to Sing" are among many musical selections that can work using this mind skill.

Did you snicker at "Row, Row, Row Your Boat"? If so, think about it again. Who is in charge of rowing your boat anyway? Why not use this tune to re-mind yourself that you row your own boat? And examine the phrase "row, row, row" more carefully. Isn't it about determination and persistence? And rowing down the stream is easier than rowing up stream, right? Aren't there times when we could all re-mind ourselves about the value of going with the flow instead of fighting it? And while you're rowing, why not choose to be happy and row merrily?

COSMIC TIME

Cosmic Time, a strategy for choosing your point of per-spective, is another mind skill that can empower students and teachers alike. I have a friend who stopped by to visit during a violent thunderstorm. When he left two hours later, he found that a heavy tree limb had fallen on his car, causing consider-able damage. When he remarked, "Ten years from now no one will care," I knew he was using the mind skill of Cosmic Time to his advantage.

In situations like the one my friend encountered, most of us choose to get up real close and examine every scratch and indentation on the car. As we put the crumpled vehicle under the microscope, we make it large and see it as important, often creating the event bigger in our minds than it needs to be.

Cosmic Time is a skill that re-minds us to back up and look at the situation from a different perspective. Take a few steps back mentally and look at this car from the vantage point of one year from today. How important will the dents be then? Now, back up even further. See the car from a ten-year vantage point. Now how important are those bumps in the grand scheme of things? Use your mind to back up again and notice this situation and the significance it takes on in terms of all of time. In cosmic time, how important is it really that the car was hit with a limb today?

Use Cosmic Time to decide how to perceive any recent event. You can choose to get up close and make it big and seem important, or you can back up, see it in terms of cosmic time, and make it small and less significant. Is the event insignificant or critical? It's both and neither. It is one or the other depending on your perspective. And perspective is under your control.

LET IT GO

A third-grade teacher had students writing on toilet paper recently. No paper shortage existed. The toilet paper choice was a purposeful decision that would symbolically represent the mind skill she was currently presenting to her students.

"You each have two sheets of toilet paper," she explained. "With a pen, I want you to write a sentence describing some incident that happened this year that you would like to forget.

Perhaps it was your grade on the last spelling test, or the time Mr. Stanley had to come in to ask you to be more respectful of the substitute teacher. It could be a time you teased or were teased. Maybe you couldn't find the right birthday present for a friend or didn't get invited to a party. Take a minute and record the incident on your toilet paper."

The students did as instructed. They were used to engaging in unusual activities in this classroom. After all, their teacher was a Spirit Whisperer.

When everyone had finished writing, this educator marched her students into the restroom, where they deposited their writings in the toilet. "Watch what happens," she instructed as she flushed the toilet. As you would expect, a swirl of water swept the papers away and out of sight as the interested students crowded around to get a good view.

After the students had returned to their seats, the teacher inductively coaxed from them the messages the activity was intended to deliver, which included:

- If you don't like what's happening in your life, you can flush it.
- What's done is done. Let it go.
- Get rid of bad feelings.
- Writing it down and throwing it away helps you get rid of it.
- Don't hang on to negative thoughts.

Let It Go is the mind skill this teacher was demonstrating with the toilet paper activity. Again, this is a mind skill that can be carried out physically, using the toilet, or done with a mental flush.

Symbolic gestures and imagery help mind skills stick in the consciousness. Let It Go can be accomplished by tying messages on balloons and actually letting them go, or it can be done mentally, visualizing the balloons ascending in your imagination. Resentments from the past can be burned or buried, flushed, or sent away on balloons. They can be ripped up and thrown in the wastebasket.

The symbolism of actually burning file cards in a burn barrel and the imagery of seeing the cards and what they represent burn in your mind are right-brain activities. That's the stuff of long-term memory. What are students going to remember about your classroom 10 years from now? Probably not that one day they learned five new compound words. Probably not that they read a chapter on amphibians. Probably not that they got a "B" on the economics test. But I bet they'll never forget the day they went out on the school grounds and buried their "I can'ts." The day of the balloon launch will stick, as will the day they flushed their concerns down the toilet.

OWN IT

Own It, the final mind skill presented here, helps students take responsibility for what is happening in their lives. It reduces stress, facilitates solution seeking, and increases their sense of personal power.

Own It is a technique to use when you feel like a victim—when you're tempted to feel unfairly treated. Instead of focusing on what the other person did to you or how they created the situation you're facing, Own It by examining all the decisions you had control over, things you did to set it up, ways you contributed to the outcome, choices you had along the way. Assigning blame and finding fault are not the focus here. Responsibility is the issue. Where were you responsible in this scenario? Where could you have altered the course? Where could you have made a difference?

My travel agent once messed up on a free ticket I intended to use to fly cross-country. It looked as though her error would cost me hundreds of dollars and/or end my plans. I was livid, blaming her in my mind for being stupid, not following through, and being unprofessional. I was creating stress and immobilizing myself with blame and judgement, all of it directed at her.

Then I remembered the Own It technique. I began to look at where and how I helped create the situation. I realized that I picked this person from all the travel agents available. I was responsible for that decision. I chose not to read the back of the free ticket. I neglected to look for blackout dates. I waited until one week before the trip to check with her. I began to own the situation. No blame, fault, or guilt here. Just ownership.

As soon as I took responsibility for the situation, I calmed down. I stopped creating stress. Consequently, I was better able to enter a space of solution seeking. I called the agent back and we were able to work out an alternative plan that did cost me some dollars but enabled me to go through with my personal plans.

What are you stewing about right now? Disgusted with your principal? Upset with your students for some reason? Mad at the auto mechanic who said he could fix your car? Have a relative that you're allowing to get under your skin? Own It and see if you don't change your mind about the situation. Put this mind skill to work in your life, experience its usefulness and you'll find ways to teach it to your students.

Should mind skills be an important part of a child's education? Yes. Learning to use your mind to choose your perception of events, let go of frustrations, make a fresh start, or take responsibility for your life's circumstances is critical for healthy, successful living.

True, state assessment tests and grade level achievement tests do not measure the learning or application of mind skills. Teachers are not yet held accountable for this type of instruction. Test designers, state department officials, politicians, and educational decision-makers don't appear to be mind-full of the importance of this aspect of the mind. Perhaps it's time to re-mind them.

DEVELOPING AN "I CAN" SPIRIT

Two questions Spirit Whisperers periodically ask themselves are:

- Am I helping students count their wins or their losses?
- Am I helping students see themselves as winners or losers?

Passing through the halls of a middle school in rural Nebraska, I noticed a seventh-grade student wearing a button that displayed three capital letters: ICM. Conspicuously displayed on his shirt, the button easily attracted my attention.

"What have you got there?" I asked, pointing to the button and hoping to have my curiosity satisfied.

"An ICM button," came the reply, giving me no new information and the feeling that the question was perceived as somehow unnecessary.

Undaunted, I persevered. "So what does ICM stand for?" For all I knew, it could have been Roman numerals, advertising, or an indication of a preferred candidate in a school election. It was none of these.

"I Can Manage," was the unexpected response. "My teacher gave it to me this morning."

"Really?" I continued. "What exactly can you manage?"

"I can manage my materials. Do you know that I brought a pencil, paper, and my books to class three days in a row?"

"Well, congratulations," I offered, and then secured directions on how to find the teacher who passes out ICM buttons to students who can manage.

Avril Harris taught a self-contained class of middle school special education students. The young man I approached in the corridor was one of her students who had indeed been recently recognized and decorated for his efforts at managing materials. She opened a desk drawer and showed me several other ICM buttons, which she used to honor students who demonstrate management skills.

"I give them for a variety of management issues," she explained. "Managing time, priorities, and materials are all appropriate. I gave one out last week to a young lady who was learning to manage her mouth. Once I gave one to a student who managed to keep his hands and feet to himself for an extended period of time. My goal here, obviously, is to get these students to focus on what they *can* do rather than on what they can't. I see my job as helping them to perceive themselves as students who can manage, who do exercise control, who do choose to take responsibility for themselves and their materials."

An important aspect of the ICM button experience is the involvement of other adults in the building. Teachers, cooks, custodians, secretaries, and administrators have all been instructed by Avril to approach any student wearing an ICM button and do intentionally what I had done accidentally. Their job is to inquire, "Hey, what did you get that for?" As a result, several times a day the student has an opportunity to announce aloud, "I can manage my materials." Repetitiously, throughout the day, he can verbally affirm his self-management skills.

I don't think there are ICM buttons for teachers who can manage to help children focus on their positive efforts at self-management, but if there were, a Spirit Whisperer who teaches special education students in Nebraska would be wearing one today.

These are some other ways in which Spirit Whisperers can help students count their successes.

- Have students keep "I Can" journals, where they record and keep a permanent record of things they can do.
- Place an "I Can" container on each student's desk. When a goal is achieved or a "can" accomplished, add a slip of paper marking the event to the container.
- Construct a Proud Line (clothesline) across your room. Display things students can do. Add one of yours.
- Stretch an "I Can" chain across your room and have students add a link every time they identify a new "can."
- Invite students to bring a Success Object from home that is tangible proof of their success with some endeavor. A Success Object could be a ribbon, certificate, trophy, medal, etc. If they don't have one, help them design one. Put them on display.
- Use your camera to record major accomplishments and display them in a photo collection. Any time a child does something for the first time, capture the event and preserve it in your class book.

Helping students count their wins is a way to help them see visible, tangible proof of their unlimited potential and to develop affirming self-talk that supports that view.

If you happened to be downtown around 10:30 in the morning in a small Michigan community not too long ago, you might have been handed a sheet of paper by a teenager that read:

YOUR LIFE OR POLLUTION

Your life or pollution, one of them is going to win. If you think that pollution will never take over, you could be wrong.

Right this very minute, a chemical extract from fertilizer could be eating up your liver, giving you cancer, or causing birth defects. There are a lot more pollution problems like this that are dangerous to your health.

If we don't start taking serious action right now, we are going to wipe ourselves out. If you're concerned, as I am, please get a piece of paper and pencil and write to your senator. See if he can help stop factories from dumping chemicals in our lakes and rivers. Thank you for your help.

Sarah Remington

If you escaped being approached by Sarah Remington passing out her position paper on pollution, chances are one of the other eighth-graders would have nailed you with one of theirs. Forty students roamed the streets of this small town that morning in search of adults, looking for possible recipients for their writings.

This project was the culminating activity of a unit on pollution operated by two team-teaching Spirit Whisperers whose philosophy was not to "teach" government, but rather to let students "live" government. A main objective of this project was to have these students come to the belief that government works and that they as youngsters can have some degree of influence. The teaching team wanted them to finish the project with the feeling that I CAN DO SOMETHING.

Weeks earlier, students studied pollution by listening to Lecture Bursts, watching videos, listening to tapes, and reading articles. They completed worksheets, took tests, and participated in class discussions.

Once these students became informed concerning the issue of pollution, they were challenged by their teachers to do something about it. One of the options was to write a position paper to be handed out in the community. Several students chose this option.

Students who chose the position paper were required to create a piece of writing that contained no grammatical or spelling errors. Papers were rewritten as many times as it was necessary to eliminate them. Final drafts were completed and copied for distribution.

Before heading downtown to share the writings with the community, students discussed what situations could develop. What do you do if someone gets angry and yells at you? How should you respond to indifference? "Do's" and "don'ts" were role-played. Courtesy was stressed and practiced.

Parental permission slips were required and collected.

Students and teachers walked the 10 blocks to the downtown area. In groups of two or three, students were assigned a distribution spot. The bank, post office, and stores were all covered. Students were expected to stay at their assigned posts until instructed to leave.

The community reaction to this activity was varied, some of it negative. The responses students reported included:

- "No thanks. I don't need any more trash."
- "If you're so concerned about pollution, why don't you go pick up that can over there?"

- "Why aren't you in school learning something?"
- One storeowner questioned the students' right to use his sidewalk without permission.
- One citizen took the paper, flipped a cigarette butt onto the sidewalk, and proceeded into the post office.
- A businessman approached a teacher and pointed out a spelling error.

But the students' distribution of their position papers also met with positive responses, such as a local banker's offer to come to school and share what he knew about pollution.

These teachers knew, as most of you know, that these students were learning something. Each one of these young adults had chosen to take a stand on an issue of importance to him or her. Each had chosen to risk themselves and their views in public. Each learned that one of the best ways to come to believe that I CAN DO SOMETHING is simply to go out and do something.

Later that day, a group of Camp Fire Girls was observed picking up trash in the park. It was no coincidence that their leader had been downtown earlier that day and had received three of the position papers. She had heard the message and was passing it on. It seems that I CAN DO SOMETHING is a message that is contagious.

VISUALIZATION

Another strategy Spirit Whisperers use to implement the Principle of Personal Power is that of positive picturing. Visualization is an incredibly powerful learning tool.

If you don't believe in the power of images, interview an advertising executive and ask her if images can influence behavior. Spirit Whisperers teach their students to use imagery on their own behalf to help them achieve personal goals. Teaching students to mentally picture a desired outcome helps them to focus on the end results they desire rather than on the problem. If you can see it in your mind, you have a better chance of accomplishing it. Images do teach.

Jarrett McLoud and Lisa Oberlin teach in the same school district in an affluent suburb of a major city. Jarrett is a high school science teacher and president of his teachers' union. He's a 20-year teaching veteran who believes that his role of professional educator includes speaking out for teachers' rights. Lisa teaches second grade. She is a new hire, in her third year, and has not yet been granted tenure. She attends her professional association meetings if they don't interfere with her home life but does not assume an active role in that organization.

Although Jarrett and Lisa differ in years of experience, grade level taught, and commitment to the local and national education associations, they have at least one thing in common. Both believe that one important element related to achievement is the ability to picture the desired outcome in your mind. Both use the technique with students to increase achievement and create mental models of desired behavior.

"Just put your heads down on your desks for a minute," Lisa tells her second-graders moments before they're due in the all-purpose room for an assembly. "Rest a minute and relax. See if you can hear yourself breathe. Now I want you to use your imagination to create some pictures in your mind.

"Can you see me up in front of the class? Good. Now hear me call for us to line up for the assembly. Watch as you walk quietly over to the door and get in line. Notice that you have chosen someone to stand next to that will help you listen to the speaker when we get to the gym.

"See our class walking down the hall to the assembly. See how quietly and orderly we walk as a class. The first-graders don't even look up as we pass their open door. Feel proud and smile to yourself.

"Now see yourself sitting in the gym enjoying the assembly. Notice how you keep your eyes on the speaker and sit quietly, thinking about the message she is sharing with us. Hear yourself applaud when it's over. Again, use your imagination to see the orderly exit and flow of our class back to the classroom. Notice how you go directly to your seat and sit up alert, ready to talk about what we just heard. Now, when you're ready, sit up and let's line up for the assembly."

This kind of mental run-through of an event helps children get a clear picture of what the teacher expects. It creates a mental model of the desired behavior in their minds. It provides them with the opportunity to see themselves doing what is expected and to experience positive feelings about it. That the experience is imagined doesn't matter. What children can imagine, hold in their minds, and see themselves doing they can achieve.

Spirit Whisperers believe that children won't act properly in the hall unless they have a picture in their minds of what acting properly in the hall looks like. Children won't read smoothly without interruptions unless they can see themselves doing just that. And students will not exercise alternatives to fighting unless they can visualize those alternatives. Without pictures in their minds of what alternatives look like, how can students possibly choose them, Spirit Whisperers wonder?

Practicing something in your head can be as effective as physical practice. Arnold Palmer, the well-known golfer, never hits a shot until he approaches the ball, stands over it, and mentally pictures his swing, the flight of the ball, and a positive outcome of the effort. If you're not able to see yourself doing something, chances are you won't do it well.

Repetitious positive picturing is a strong agent in helping people achieve their goals. The ability to visualize what you want is a big step toward achieving it. Spirit Whisperers help students take that step.

Jarret McLoud uses positive picturing to assist his science students to learn and recall important curricular concerns.

"Just kick back," he announces. "I'm going to take you on a trip through your digestive system, using your imagination. If you want to close your eyes you can, but you don't have to. Just relax and let your imagination take over.

"Your body's process of extracting useful nutrients from food is called digestion. Today, you are going to take a trip through your own body and see how the digestive system works. You'll be using your mind to travel through a whole group of organs that change food into soluble products that your body can use.

"Digestion begins in the mouth, so let's start there. Imagine yourself in a protective capsule inside your mouth. You can see out and observe what is happening. Watch now, as food enters your mouth. It could be pizza or salad or your favorite sandwich. Notice how your teeth tear into it, breaking it into smaller pieces. See your teeth cutting and chopping the food into still smaller pieces. Now notice the tongue. Watch as your tongue mixes the food particles with a juice that helps moisten it. This juice is called saliva. Watch as the moistened and chopped food starts down a tube called the esophagus. See a little flap there that keeps the windpipe closed while food is swallowed. That's the epiglottis."

The imaginary journey continues through the stomach, small and large intestines, colon, and rectum until the food is absorbed by the body and/or expelled as excrement. Throughout the Lecture Burst, Jarret invites students to engage their minds and their senses to visualize, taste, and hear the work being done by the digestive system.

Well-schooled as a professional science educator, Jarret McLoud is familiar with brain research. He knows that the brain is divided into two hemispheres. The left side is the logical, rational, linear, verbal part of our brain. Much of what is done in traditional education addresses the left side of the brain. The right side is the part that is intuitive, imaginative, and holistic. It deals with pictures and is programmed through the imagination. This is the part of our brain that is often left out in typical classroom procedures. Jarret believes that for students to get the maximum effect of the curriculum he's expected to deliver, and to increase their levels of achievement, he needs to teach to both sides of the brain. That's why he uses the technique of positive picturing.

Whether their goal is to make behavioral expectations clear or to move complicated concepts into long-term memory, Spirit Whisperers at all grade levels across the county use the technique of positive picturing to engage mental rehearsal. It is their belief that it helps students reach their goals, maximize their potential, and increase their sense of personal power.

THE POWER OF CHOICE

Dr. Gonzales teaches math in Southern California. He sees his role as one not of giving students power but of helping them tap into and use the power that already exists within each one of them. Whether he knows it or not, he's a Spirit Whisperer.

Dr. Gonzales's ninth-grade algebra students were used to the routine. Each day they were greeted by a smiling teacher and five rows of six desks each. They entered the room quietly, went straight to their assigned seats, took out their homework, and looked to the board for any special directions. Clear expectations had created the norm, and two months of repeating those behaviors had locked them in place. So it was with considerable surprise and curiosity that these students entered their classroom on the third day of November.

This day, the precisely structured rows were gone. Six desks and chairs, arranged in a circle, occupied the center of the room. They faced inward. The remaining desks and chairs, including Dr. Gonzales's, lined the walls of this algebra classroom.

As students entered they stopped, did a double take, displayed a puzzled look, and moved on into the classroom. The desks and chairs that butted up against the classroom walls were the first to be occupied. Whispers and soft laughter greeted the students who arrived shortly before the tardy bell. Finding all but the chairs in the center taken, they chose to stand around the outside. No one took a seat in the center of the classroom.

"It looks a little bit different in here today," Dr. Gonzales began. "That's because we're going to do something we've not done before."

"I need some volunteers," he continued. "I'd like six of you to take the seats in the middle."

"What do we have to do?" one of the standing students asked.

"I'm not going to tell you until I get six volunteers, but I will tell you that you'll be able to handle it. So who would be willing to take a risk and help us out?"

Most professional educators know the value of wait time. They also know how long a minute can seem when the clock is moving and there is an absence of dialogue or action. Dr. Gonzales waited for one minute, then repeated his request. He waited another minute, then spoke again. It took several repetitions of this process and six minutes before the first student stepped forward. After eight minutes all six chairs were filled with willing, if somewhat skeptical, algebra students.

Dr. Gonzales then addressed the students sitting in the outside ring. "Please take out your journals and pencils. Here's what I want you to do. Closely observe your classmates sitting in the center. Record what you see them doing. Write down behavior, body language, posture, anything that is observable. What do you see? Keep recording until I give the signal to stop."

Immediately pencils moved across the journal pages, recording observations such as:

- Slouched, legs out in front
- Looking down at the floor
- Shoulders drooped
- Silly grins
- Looking around
- Puzzled faces
- Shifting around in the seat
- I saw one person who looked sort of rigid.

As the journal recording continued, Dr. Gonzales directed his remarks to the students who had volunteered to sit in the middle. "You don't know what I'm going to ask you to do, do you?" he asked.

"No," they responded.

"Well, I'm not going to tell you exactly what it is, but I want you to pretend like you know what it is and that you feel confident you can do it."

"But what is it?" one of the volunteers wanted to know.

"It doesn't matter what it is. Just act as if you know you can do it."

As the volunteers began to follow the directions, a dramatic shift in behavior and corresponding journal entries occurred. Recorded observations this time included:

- I saw people sit up straight.
- Legs went under the desk.
- Eyes looked forward.
- One person smiled.
- Chests seemed to expand.
- Everybody shifted.
- People looked at each other.
- They seemed more alert.

After two minutes had elapsed, Dr. Gonzales called time. He then led a discussion kicked off with the questions, "What did you see the people in the center do? What behaviors did you see before I gave them instructions?"

Students shared eagerly what was written in their journals in response to the first observation period. Most observations were descriptive. "I saw looking away." "I noticed Bill had his hands in his pocket the entire time." Other comments included inferences. "I noticed a lack of confidence." "Most of them looked scared."

When Dr. Gonzales's questions and the discussion turned to behaviors observed and recorded following the second set of instructions, the comments were quite different. "They all sat up straight." "I think they were more confident." "They started looking around the room and at each other." "It didn't look like the same group."

When asked about their reactions, the volunteers reported, "I felt better the second time." "I didn't know what you wanted at first, so I just sat there." "I felt tense until you said to pretend like we knew."

After listening to and reflecting on several student responses, Dr. Gonzales shared his own interpretation and explanation of the activity. The Spirit Whisperer in him started to come out as he explained, "I watched all of you yesterday when you took the chapter test. Some of you sat slumped in your chairs seconds after you came in. Others sat up straight and alert. Some fidgeted with pencils, keys, and hair. Some looked down, some straight ahead. A few of you even smiled. It was clear to me that some of you were acting confident. Others appeared nervous. And I hadn't even passed out the test yet. Without having seen it, you were all into your act.

"Think of it this way," he suggested. "Many times in our lives we face new experiences, a fresh challenge, an event that we haven't dealt with before. When you approach that experience, you don't really know if you can do it or not. No one knows for sure until they do it. You might think that you could or even believe that you could. Those are helpful thoughts and beliefs, but you still don't know for sure. Not until you do it.

"When approaching a test, a new responsibility, a set of directions being read for the first time, you all have a choice. You can act as if you can or you can act as it you can't. You can pretend like you'll be able to handle it, or pretend like you won't. That choice is up to you.

"Who do you think will learn a foreign language sooner, the person acting confident or the one acting scared? And when you take drivers' training, which act do you think would be more helpful? In each case the choice is yours. And you get to make that choice many times throughout the day.

"Those are my thoughts on the activity that we did today. Now I invite you to share some of yours with me," Dr. Gonzales concluded.

A five-minute period of reflective writing put the final touch on a lesson that would reach further into these students' lives than any mathematical instruction they were expecting.

Just before the bell rang, Dr. Gonzales shared one more important piece of information with his students. "By the way," he said, "we'll be taking that chapter test over tomorrow. When you come through this door, make a conscious choice of how to act. See you all tomorrow."

Dr. Gonzales was empowering his students by helping them appreciate the fact that they choose their act. Many students aren't aware that they choose their act. Until they become conscious of the act they're choosing and realize they have control over it, chances are they won't change.

An act often chosen by students at a variety of grade levels is the "I can't" act. The words that accompany "I can't" behaviors often have a whiny ring. Watch and listen for this act. Soon, one of your students will look at you and respond, "I can't do it."

You might hear "I can't" from a fifth-grader examining a page full of fractions. Perhaps a five-year-old attempting to tie his own shoes will utter those words. Or maybe your fifth-hour honor student will say, "I can't," in response to a challenging assignment. Whatever the circumstance, your response is critical.

The typical teacher/parent response to "I can't" is "Sure you can. Come on, try." We use those words with the best of intentions, to offer encouragement and share our belief that we know the student could do it if they would just try. The problem is that the words don't work. They don't work because *trying* doesn't work. Only *doing* works. Trying is a cop-out. Anyone busy trying is someone not busy doing.

If you think trying is important, I challenge you to go up in an airplane with someone who is going to "try" to land it. Or perhaps you'd like to have a heart transplant from someone who is going to "try" to transfer the heart successfully. My preference is to be with someone who will do more than try. I want a doctor and an airline pilot who will *do it*.

The next time someone looks at you and says, "I can't do it," look them in the eye and say simply, "Act as if you can."

The typical student response to this directive is "Huh?"

Then say it again. "Act as if you can. Act as if you have done this 10 times already." Then go somewhere else in your classroom. Move to the other side of the room and observe from there.

"Act as if you can" won't work with every student, and it won't work every time. Yet, I predict this "I can't" antidote will pleasantly surprise you.

Other ways to say, "Act as if you can," are "Pretend," "Play like you can," and "Fake it till you make it." Each is an effort to get students to stay conscious of the act they are choosing and give them an opportunity to choose differently. If you're not sure these "I can't" antidotes will work with your students, why not act as if they will?

"We can't go on." That was the "I can't" language that seventh-grade language arts teacher Betty Wing heard from a student in one of her cooperative learning groups recently.

"I don't understand," she responded, as her eye contact extended to include everyone in the group.

"We don't know what to do next. We can't go on," explained another group member.

At this point, Betty could have chosen from a variety of responses available to her. Answers that would have given students in this peer-editing group the information they were seeking include:

- "Make sure you recheck the spelling."

- "Reread the section on how to use quotation marks."
- "Move on to the next student's paper."

But Betty chose not to answer the group's question. She purposefully chose to ignore the content specifics of the question and instead crafted her reply to address a bigger issue, one of personal power. "If you did know what to do next, what would you do?" she asked.

After a brief period of silence, one student in the group came up with an answer. Responding to the suggestion provided from within their own group, these students quickly returned to the task at hand. Satisfied that the group was now moving along, Betty positioned herself to observe another group.

Betty's response to the "We can't go on. What are we supposed to do next?" attitude of this group was not an accident. It was created by her intention to help students experience a concept held in high regard by Spirit Whisperers: *As an empowered individual in an autonomous group, there are alternatives to seeking help from the teacher.*

Had Betty answered the question by suggesting the group turn to page 63, or had she given these students three alternatives from which to choose, she would have sent the silent message, "Don't trust yourself. Teachers know. Students don't." By asking instead "If you did know, what would you do next?" this Spirit Whisperer made herself dispensable and helped her seventh-graders access their own power.

Workshop participants often ask, "What if she 'acts as if' and begins doing it wrong? What if he pretends like he has done it before and he still doesn't quite have it?" In the scenario above, students in the group chose a "next" response that was incorrect. Their choice was not what they were supposed to do next. This is not a cause for worry. Acting "as if" doesn't get students doing things perfectly, but it does get them *doing*. You and they can adjust from there. Ever try to steer a parked car? Difficult, indeed. Get the car moving and the steering becomes a bit easier. "Act as if," "pretend," "play like," and "fake it till you make it" are intended to get the car moving.

The fastest way to help others experience personal power in their lives is to allow them to make as many choices as are feasible as early as possible, taking safety, health, and practicality into consideration. Spirit Whisperers allow. They allow choice, input in decisions, mistakes, and correction. They also allow students to experience the legitimate consequences of their actions.

Consequently, Spirit Whisperers refrain from telling students what to do. How can a student assume increasing levels of personal power if he is consistently being told what to do and when to do it? When the outside authority is providing direction, the inside authority withers. If you don't use it, you lose it.

Spirit Whisperers are leery of giving advice, and they approach that strategy cautiously. Only two things can happen if you give advice. The student can take it or leave it. If the student takes your advice and it works, she keeps returning to you for advice. Dependence grows. As faith in the advice giver increases, belief in self decreases. If the student takes your advice and it doesn't work, resentment flows from the student toward you, the advice giver. You lose stature in the student's eyes. If the student ignores your advice, resentment flows from the advice giver towards the student. ("I gave him a great idea and he refused to follow through; I'll be darned if I'll give him any more good ideas.")

Spirit Whisperers do not give students unsolicited advice. They see their job as helping the student generate solutions, sort through thoughts and feelings, and gain confidence through solution seeking and decision-making. They understand it is important to allow students to make some mistakes in judgement. They know that learning comes from experiencing the positive and negative consequences of decisions. They allow.

Yes, Spirit Whisperers have a responsibility to share the information they possess that will help students make informed decisions. They teach students about the dangers of smoking, the importance of wearing a seat belt, and the laws that govern each. They give necessary information on sexually transmitted diseases and job possibilities with and without a high school diploma; they explain the dangers of throwing rocks or failing to develop a wide and varied vocabulary.

Spirit Whisperers share what they know, but they do it from the position of information provider only. They do not often assume the role of advice giver. They realize that what has worked for them may or may not work for someone else. They do not impose solutions, ideas, or beliefs. They allow. They allow students to develop their own beliefs, test their own ideas, and find their own solutions. In essence, they allow students to rely on themselves.

Spirit Whisperers use Teacher Talk that prefaces suggestions with phrases that allow the child to retain responsibility.

- "How would you feel about . . .?"
- "Would you consider . . .?"
- "How would you like . . .?"

These sentence starters acknowledge that your suggestion may not be the student's best answer.

Another effort that Spirit Whisperers make to empower students is to eradicate automatic responses. Automatic responses are knee-jerk reactions to outside events. They are mental reflexes that result in physical actions, usually done without thinking. All that is needed to prompt an automatic response is an outside stimulus. The automatic response follows swiftly and predictably.

If one student grabs another's hat, the automatic response could be a fist in the face. Giving up when the problems get tougher is an automatic response for another student.

A student making automatic responses lives a life of programmed reaction rather than one of conscious creation. This student is, in effect, controlled by the outside environment. When the environment changes, her response changes. Stimulus dictates response. The student behaves like a robot, programmed by similar feelings and events of the past.

The more automatic a student's responses, the less response-ability he possesses. He is less able to make appropriate, effective responses based on his present moment reality. Automatic responses are barriers to claiming personal power and making minute to minute choices based on ever-changing data and possibilities.

To move from "react" to "create," students must learn control. Mind control, body control, impulse control, anger control are all about staying conscious and making choices. Spirit Whisperers help students learn control by helping them stay conscious. If a student is conscious, she can stop. If you stop, you can think. You can think through the consequences of your typical behavior. ("Is this behavior going to get me what I really want?" "Does it help me be who I really am?" "How do I want to 'be' here?")

If you stop, you can think of possibilities. ("What choices do I have here?") If you stop and think and generate possibilities, you can appraise them based on possible consequences. ("If I choose A, then X and Y could happen. If I choose B, then T and S are likely to occur.")

If you stop, think, and appraise, then you can choose. ("I choose to speak up for myself and share my feelings.")

Personal power is not found in the actions of others. It is claimed in our reactions to the actions of others. If you stop, think, appraise, and choose, then you are in control of how you want to be and what you want to do. You are not at the mercy of automatic responses. You have response-ability.

One goal of this chapter is to increase teacher awareness of the number and type of tools available for implementing the Principle of Personal Power. As the saying goes, if the only tool you have is a hammer, you tend to look at everything as if it were a nail. If you believe students need to have power "done to" them, you'll likely use your hammer to pound away at them.

One problem with "doing power" to students is that it encourages a hammer fight. You get out your hammer, so they bring out a bigger one. You use an even bigger hammer and students up-level the conflict with a hammer that is bigger still. Since the one with the biggest hammer wins, and adults have bigger hammers than students do, you eventually win. But do you?

No one really wins a hammer fight, and no one wins a power struggle with a student. You may win a battle, but the student lives to fight another day. Even if you activate one of your biggest hammers and suspend a student from school for two weeks, there he is two weeks later, sitting in that fourth chair in the second row.

The only way to win a power struggle is to make sure it comes out win/win. If you win and students lose, you lose. If students win and you lose, they lose. No one wins if someone else loses. Spirit Whisperers understand the concept of win/win and work to achieve it in their classrooms. That is one of the ways in which they implement the material contained in the next chapter, "The Principle of Oneness."

CHAPTER 6

The Principle of Oneness

In a first-grade gifted, pullout program, 17 student desks are scattered around a large early childhood classroom. When asked why the desks are so far apart, the teacher replies, "These are gifted children. You know a key characteristic of gifted children is their strong verbal ability. If I don't keep them apart, they'll talk all the time."

A parent enrolling his child in a middle school was informed by the principal that his daughter would need a backpack as part of her school supplies. At this school students are required to carry all their books from class to class throughout the day. When questioned about whether the students had lockers and if books could be kept there, the principal smiled and informed this parent, "We have lockers, but students can use them only before and after school. Students don't have time to go to their lockers between classes because we only allow them three minutes to pass from one class to the next. We used to give students six minutes, but we found out all they do is use that time to talk to their friends."

A fourth-grade student works independently on his green level SRA spelling card. When he completes that task he moves on to an individualized math program, where he has zoomed 27 pages ahead of all his classmates. Later he works on an individual report for science and then proceeds to a reading program where he moves along at a speed consistent with his own abilities. In computer class he sits in front of a computer and works steadily through the workbook at his own pace.

Walking the corridors of a high school not far from my home, I'm struck by the silence of the classrooms. In room after room I see students with their noses to the grindstone, reading, writing, perhaps thinking. On occasion, I hear a teacher's voice. Students sit quietly.

It seems that never in the history of our educational system have we invested so heavily to bring students together so we can keep them separated.

Recently I was approached by a concerned student teacher at a staff development program I conducted. Results she had obtained from a university assignment troubled her. As part of her final university education class her task was to pick one high school student, follow the student around school for a day, and write up a paper detailing a day in the life of that particular student.

The student teacher had just completed the assignment and was disturbed by the results of her observations. She had chosen a 15-year-old girl to shadow and was startled to find that no one spoke to that student during the entire day. Not one other student. Not one teacher. Not one human being spoke to this high school student at any time during the day. Not in class. Not in the hall. Not in the lunchroom. Not in the media center. Nowhere. No one. Not even once.

In a suburban middle school a transfer student enrolled several weeks after school had begun. His father told me that after 10 weeks in the new school his son had made one friend.

"How can you be in a middle school for 10 weeks and make only one friend?" I inquired.

The father, a professional educator himself, did some checking. What he discovered was that this school had no provisions for welcoming new students. There was no "buddy" system. There was no one to check up on a new student to see if he was getting his locker open. There was no one to make sure he had someone to sit with during lunch. There was no support group, no homeroom program, no advisory concept where connectedness and bonding are encouraged. There were few opportunities to work with other students and create connections.

Sense of family, intimacy, and feelings of belonging were clearly not priorities in the schools described in the scenarios above.

Are these isolated incidents? Is the high school student who went the whole day without being spoken to merely an extreme case? Is the student who made only one friend totally responsible for making his own friends? Schools are not supposed to be concerned with students getting their social needs met anyway, are they?

The answers to these questions depend on who you want to be. They depend on what you want your school to be. And they depend on how you see yourself in relation to others.

Separateness occurs in schools where the prevailing perception is that others are separate from me, disconnected. In a school where the predominant belief is that everyone else is an extension of me, a part of me, there is less separation, less isolation, less tolerance for emotional hurt and pain.

Fifth-grade teacher Charles Harrington was challenged to put his beliefs about interconnectedness and the Principle of Oneness into practice recently. His challenge came without warning. Charles was strumming his guitar when it happened. His fifth-graders were singing Civil War songs, experiencing the sounds and words characteristic of that period in American history. No one expected it. There appeared to be no reason for it. Loud and clear it resonated throughout the room. "You pig!" one student shouted at another.

Charles stopped strumming. The students stopped singing. All eyes turned to the teacher. "Jason, that's a put-down," he began. "Put-downs violate the responsible action statements that we live by in fifth grade. What we do in fifth grade when we're angry is tell the other person how we're feeling and what we would like to have happen. Please share your feelings in words that respect both yourself and Madison."

Charles Harrington does not allow put-downs in his classroom. "What you do to one, you've done to all," he tells his students. They're learning they can express their feelings and communicate effectively without putting each other down. Slowly, they're beginning to understand and live the Principle of Oneness.

Imagine a classroom, a school, a world where everyone acted as if they were part of a greater whole, where everyone saw themselves as part of something larger than themselves. Imagine what a school would be like if people behaved as if they were connected, as if they perceived a blow or a benefit to one as a blow or a benefit to all?

Wouldn't it be difficult to hurt another if you saw your action as hurting yourself? How could the hurt feel good if what you did unto others you were actually doing unto yourself? Wouldn't it be easier to treat your neighbor as you would treat yourself if you saw your neighbor as part of your self?

You might be thinking this type of learning isn't for educational institutions. This stuff is too spiritual. This is not our business. We're educators, not spiritual leaders. This is definitely outside the boundaries of our job.

But is it? Is it outside the boundaries of our job to help students appreciate that everything is interconnected, that all of life is interwoven into patterns of interdependence and unity? Is it inconsistent with what it means to be a professional educator to help students learn that everything we do—every choice we make—affects everything else in the universe? Is the notion that no man is an island not a concept worthy of teaching?

Spirit Whisperers are spiritual leaders. Spirit Whisperers know that separateness is an illusion. They work to help students appreciate the interconnectedness of all things, including each other. Quietly, with whispers, they are transforming the world by putting the Principle of Oneness into practice in their classrooms.

Spirit Whisperers do not see themselves and their students as separate. They see everyone in the classroom as part of a larger whole. They perceive the strength in unity, connectedness, oneness, and strive to create it in their classrooms. Their efforts are geared toward creating a sense of family, strong feelings of belonging, and an "Our Classroom" atmosphere. (This concept is covered in depth in a previous book, *Our Classroom: We Can Learn Together*, which I co-authored with Dee Dishon.)

Interdependence is a hallmark of a Spirit Whisperer's classroom. The atmosphere is one of shared commitments and decision-making, looking for common ground, and mutual respect for one another. Teachers in these classrooms set out to intentionally create a strong sense of connectedness. They work to uplift individual spirits by building class spirit.

Add-ons are one strategy Spirit Whisperers use to build a sense of unity in their classrooms. An add-on is a product begun by the teacher, with students expected to add on their own unique contribution. One example is the "A friend is . . ." graffiti board observed in a middle school classroom. The teacher displayed the caption and made the initial contribution. Students added on and filled the poster board with their individual perceptions of what a friend is.

An add-on could be a goal-setting chain with a link that holds each student's individual goal. It could be flowers in a flowerbed, stars in the sky, grapes in a bunch, or teeth in a smile. Students may be invited to add a prediction, a sentence, an opinion, a question, or a statistic.

Add-ons give visual proof of an individual's place within the group. When displayed, they provide continuous visual impact to the notion that it takes all of us to make up our group, and everyone in our group is an important link. Having your individual contribution displayed as a grape in the bunch or a bird in the flock helps you see connectedness and your place in something larger than yourself.

Judy Bloomingdale uses the add-on technique by having her second-graders make class books. She begins the activity by assigning a topic such as "My favorite sandwich" or "Grandpas and Grandmas." Students write and illustrate their reactions to the topic. After each individual contribution is ready, holes are punched and the pages are fastened together with metal rings. The result is a class book produced by the students for the students. Class books are displayed in the classroom library and are checked out using the same procedure that students use to check out regular library books.

A seventh-grade teacher invites her language arts students to add contractions to the contraction chain. They also contribute to the compound word file and the list of troublesome spelling words.

A U.S. history teacher has students add dates to the class timeline. Dates that can be added include significant events in U.S. history and important events from the students' own lives.

Creating group products is another strategy essential to promoting unity and connectedness. Working on a class mural helps the group to bond. So does producing a class newsletter to be sent home to parents, building and tending a butterfly garden in front of the school, and creating a classroom exhibit for open house. Producing a class play and presenting it for other classrooms brings the presenting students closer together.

Were you ever involved in a high school play? Did you attend the party following the final presentation? If you did, you were probably caught up in strong feelings of caring, intimacy, and connectedness. There is something about a public performance—taking a shared risk together in front of an audience—that binds people together. Band, choir, orchestra, and athletic teams often produce strong feelings of unity for students who choose these high school experiences.

It is no accident that most cooperative learning models require students within each group to produce a single, group product. If everyone in the group is creating their own individual product, what reason is there to work together? Creating group products builds team pride, fosters feelings of belonging, and gives students a real reason to work together.

One elementary school has each class make a class flag. Students talk about the symbols that are typically found on flags and what those symbols represent. They research flags of several states and countries looking for ideas. They examine such questions as, Who are we as a classroom and what do we want to stand for? What do we want to communicate to the rest of the school about who and what we are? What are we saying about ourselves by the symbols we choose to place on our class flag?

Consensus seeking produces the symbols and final design of each room flag. Upon completion, the flags are used as a signal to come in from recess. If you're out on the playground and you see someone waving your class flag, you know that it's time to head back to the classroom.

The creation of group goals also helps build classroom unity. A group goal could be a dollar amount that is needed to finance the spring trip for the Spanish Club. It could be seeing if your entire class can get 400 spelling words correct when they take the spelling test this Friday. Having every student learn their times tables by November first, shutting out the opponent in Tuesday's game, getting all permission slips in by Thursday, and getting a "ONE" rating by the lunchroom supervisor three days in a row are further examples of group goals.

Working toward a common goal helps people pull together. The more difficult the goal, the greater the feelings of accomplishment and unity that occur when it's reached.

A first-grade teacher and her class set a group goal of accumulating 1,000 bottle caps. This teacher wanted to give her students a hands-on appreciation for what 1,000 of something actually looked and felt like. She could have easily brought in 1,000 pins or 1,000 pennies for the students to touch and view. But she knew how the excitement would build as they passed each hundred mark on their way to 1,000 and the satisfaction that is gained from pulling together to accomplish a shared goal.

Selecting a class name is another way to produce bonding, unity, and feelings of togetherness. Group validation occurs when your class becomes Snyder's Spiders, Olsen's Owls, the Pink Panthers, the Banana Splits, or the Third Hour Hummers. The specific name matters less than its use and the process of selection.

You could choose to name your class the Southwest Scientists or the History Hunters. If you alone decide on the class name, you bypass students' participation in the selection process. When you decide on a class name without student input, the name is now your name, for your class, decided by you. Attachment to a class name, pride in being part of that group, and feelings of oneness are heightened if students participate in the selection process.

Involving students in the process of name suggestion, narrowing, consensus seeking, and final selection requires more time than deciding by yourself. Yet it is just that process of involvement that builds commitment for and attachment to the final selection.

Once the class name has been selected, it can be used on other group products that validate groupness. It can be added to the class flag, song, banner, T-shirt, badge, or creed. The History Hunters can design a logo for class stationery and develop a class motto that goes with it. They can send home a monthly "History Hunter News." They can display their findings in the History Hunter display case in the hall.

When I present this material to a K-6 audience, I rarely get resistance. Naming their class, creating a class flag, making T-shirts, logos, and class stationery sound reasonable to elementary school teachers. High school teachers, on the other hand, sometimes scoff at these suggestions, although they acknowledge that business and industry invest in logos, slogans, rallies, and other strategies that build unity within a company and recognition for a brand name.

"This is Mickey Mouse stuff," a high school teacher once told me during a presentation. "My students would laugh me right out of the building if I tried to do some of these things. They're not all that important anyway," I was informed.

If a sense of belonging is not important to teenagers, then why is it that nobody is better at building unity than gangs are? Think about it. Gangs have colors, names, territory, language, rituals, jackets, handshakes, initiation ceremonies, insignias.

Ever try to get a kid out of a gang? It's not easy. The bonding and connectedness that membership in a gang represents works like cement to hold that youngster firmly within the group. Gangs know about our need to belong, to feel connected, to be part of something larger than our isolated selves. Gangs don't see these strategies as "Mickey Mouse stuff."

Coaches, too, use many of these bonding strategies to help individuals become a team. A high school football coach told me his defense is named the Junk Yard Dogs, the offense is called the Silver Stretch, and the members of the special teams refer to themselves as the Set Up Crew. They even have a name for the spectators: the Extra Ingredient. Spectators wear Extra Ingredient buttons and Extra Ingredient T-shirts. It seems that even spectators enjoy being a part of the team.

Varsity Club members at this school are encouraged to wear the varsity sweaters on game days. Spirit rallies are held. School colors are displayed along with slogans and banners. They even have a school mascot that runs around in a funny costume.

The football team's motto is: "Oneness leads to won-ness." "We win or lose together," the coach likes to remind (re-mind) his players.

In addition, his team performs the same ritual before every game. They huddle together and shout the team motto.

As they sprint onto the field, they all leap and touch the printed sign that hangs over the locker room door: "There is no "I" in team." Apparently, creating a sense of family with his players is as important to this coach as it is to gang leaders.

Another group validation technique and strategy used by Spirit Whisperers to foster the Principle of Oneness is participating in projects that help others. Raking the leaves or planting a garden for an elderly couple, sending cards and letters to a serviceman or servicewoman, cleaning up the playground, visiting a nursing home, and organizing a welcome wagon to assist new students are examples.

Performing a service—giving to others—builds connectedness. A shared sense of purpose combined with reaching out to others will help your students to connect and work as one. In addition to building unity within your class, the individuals within the group build bridges and connect to the community, the neighborhood, the elderly, and the less fortunate, as well as to the environment.

A kindergarten class adopted a grandparent as a class project. A physical education teacher organized his sixth-graders to help younger children learn to throw and catch. Many high schools today have a service requirement for graduation. Each student is expected to perform several hours of community service before receiving a diploma.

Doing projects that help others has merit in and of itself. Extending those projects by inviting students to think about them, talk about them, and write about them can add greater impact to the activity. I suggest that these service projects be regularly and thoroughly debriefed. (See Chapter 2 for a full explanation of debriefing.)

A high school student who boards her horse at the same barn I do approached me and asked if she could clean my horse's stall for a couple of weeks. To my surprise, she was willing to do this at no expense to me. All I had to do was sign a card from one of her high school classes that verified she had performed a service. I agreed.

Several weeks later I asked her about the class and how the projects had turned out. The student didn't know and she was unable to articulate what any of the other students had done for their projects. "We didn't talk about it," she informed me.

"You never talked about what you learned from the projects, or drew any conclusions?" I asked.

"No, we just had to turn in the cards with 20 hours on them."

Her teacher missed an important opportunity to cement what his students had learned. With debriefing, he could have helped them clarify the personal meanings gained from one spirit reaching out to another.

Class meetings can be used to activate the Principle of Oneness. Meetings such as the one conducted by Jason Roberts described in Chapter 5 about how to deal with the running and pushing that was taking place around the drinking fountain help students realize that solutions to problems can be found by working together. Solution seeking puts students and teacher on the same side and reinforces the value of group cohesiveness, which grows as students improve their ability to work together. The more a class pulls together to make decisions and solve problems, the more clearly they see themselves not only as a unit, but as a problem-solving, solution-seeking unit. What a healthy way for a classroom full of young people to picture themselves.

In every school there are some students who appear to be isolates. They have few friends and spend much of their time alone. They eat by themselves, study by themselves, and walk through the halls by themselves. They are on the outside looking in and are never really a part of the action—never included in an "in" group. They appear to exist on the fringe.

From students' point of view, the number one need of kids in school today is social. From our point of view, students have many other needs that have to be addressed. But from their perspective, the main need is social acceptance. All kids want it and some will even lower productivity to get it. We've all seen examples of bright youngsters purposefully achieving less than they could in order to be liked and have friends. In their minds it's more important to be social than academic.

This social need grows and becomes strongest in the middle school years. If you're not part of an in-group by middle school, your sense of belonging and feeling of oneness suffers. Some students give up the search to belong and concentrate solely on academics. Others act out. Much of what we call "acting out" in school today is simply kids getting their social needs met. Having side conversations, passing notes, coming to class late because "I was talking to my friends at my locker" are examples.

While it's not possible for a teacher to be the primary support system for all the lonely, isolated children in school, it is feasible for them to play that role for one or two students. Spirit Whisperers do that by actively reaching out to those students who appear to lack connection and feelings of belonging. They know the isolated child often believes that no one likes him. They also know that before relationships in general can improve for this child, he has to develop a relationship with someone. He has to know that someone likes him. Guess who has the best chance of becoming that someone for the isolated child in your classroom?

One way Spirit Whisperers intentionally reach out is by informing isolated students when they have positive feelings about them. They also let these self-perceived "loners" know when they have contributed to the overall well-being and progress of the class. Telling them how their behavior benefited and affected other class members helps them see the relationship between themselves and others. These kinds of teacher-initiated experiences can help them connect—help them experience oneness.

As part of their reach-out program, Spirit Whisperers share their interests, hobbies, activities, and family experiences with their students. Rather than asking questions about a student's interests and hobbies, which is often perceived as interrogation, they concentrate on making statements about themselves. They reach out through sharing themselves. Students who are receptive respond by continuing the dialogue.

Journals are another technique used by Spirit Whisperers to connect with students. Students make daily journal entries and the teacher reads them and responds in writing. The main goal of journal use in this context is relationship building. It's an effort to ensure that dialogue exists between the teacher and student. Many low-connectedness students will communicate on paper what seems too intimate to them to say aloud.

Spirit Whisperers have learned to be nonjudgmental when responding in writing to students' journal entries. They also listen without judgement when students speak aloud. They have learned not to continually correct students, nor do they feel the need to respond to everything students say. They concentrate instead on listening and on simply being there.

Another way in which Spirit Whisperers reach out to isolated youngsters is through touch. They show affection, concern, and caring through physical contact. A Spirit Whisperer's touch is often a pat on the back, a high-five, or a light squeeze on the shoulder. Even though some schools have a no-touch policy, Spirit Whisperers do not shy away from appropriate physical touch when they feel it is necessary.

In addition to physical touch, Spirit Whisperers touch with their eyes. They know the importance of sustained eye contact and that the eyes are the "windows to the soul." Eyes can say, "I care about you. You're important to me," or "I don't care. Right now something else is more important to me."

Early in my teaching career I would busy myself putting up board work as the fifth-graders came into the classroom to begin their day. If one of them came to me with a question or comment, I answered the question or spoke to him or her while I continued to write on the board. "After all, I can do two things at once," I thought to myself.

Indeed I did answer the students' questions while simultaneously finishing my board work tasks, but I know now that I missed opportunities to connect. Each time I continued to write while I spoke with my back turned, I lost a chance to tell the student through my behavior, "You're so important to me that I'll stop what I'm doing, turn and face you, and give you my eyes along with my full attention."

I suggest you reach out to students by giving them strong eye contact. One caution here: while you work at giving extended, direct eye contact to students, do not insist they make eye contact with you. There are cultures represented in classrooms today where eye contact with an adult is considered a sign of disrespect. Looking away from a person in authority or looking down is a way some children have been taught to respect elders. In addition, eye contact heightens intimacy. Allow the student to determine the degree of intimacy and risk that he or she is willing to engage. Give eye contact, invite eye contact, but do not require that it be returned.

Another way in which Spirit Whisperers touch students is through the purposeful use of strategic placement, sometimes referred to as "proximity behavior." Proximity behavior simply means being in the vicinity of the students you wish to influence.

Teachers are familiar with the technique in terms of classroom management. If you're lecturing in the front of the room and students are whispering quietly on the right side of the room, continue to lecture and move slowly to the right side of the room. That strategic placement often ends the disturbance.

You can use strategic placement as part of your reach-out effort with a student who needs increased connectedness. Simply be in the vicinity of that student more often than you normally would. Make a conscious choice to be around him or her and show your interest and concern by your presence.

As teachers, we spend more time in the proximity of students who give right answers, return our attention, dress neatly, help us feel good about being a teacher, and return our eye contact and smiles. We spend less time in the vicinity of students who give incorrect answers or no answers, dress down, show us little attention, and offer no eye contact or smiling faces. In short, we teachers spend more time near teacher pleasers than we do in the vicinity of students who don't appear to buy into our agenda.

I know of no teacher who does that on purpose. I know of no educator who says to himself, "I like this group of students better. They help me feel good about what I'm doing as a professional educator. I think I'll spend more time near them today." No one does this consciously. Yet, I have no doubt that we all gravitate to students who seem eager and motivated. If this assumption is true, it behooves us to consciously hang out in the proximity of those students who don't appear to connect as easily. Just being where they are helps lay the groundwork for relationship.

Another way to reach out is with a smile. We all think we do this on a regular basis, but do we really?

A student teacher told me about sitting in a second-grade classroom while the students were asking the teacher questions. The activity was an effort to create dialogue and build a relationship by providing a regularly scheduled "Ask Me" time when students could question the teacher on topics of interest to them.

One youngster inquired, "Do you love your students?"

"Oh, yes," replied the teacher. "I love you boys and girls more than anything. My heart is filled with love for every one of you. I love teaching. I love coming to school every day. My heart breaks when you get hurt. My heart shines when one of you learns something new. My heart is filled with love for all of you."

The student considered the answer for a moment and then wondered aloud, "Then how come your heart doesn't tell your face?"

Just because you feel love doesn't mean it's showing. Just because you feel happy on the inside doesn't mean you're smiling on the outside. Smile with intention. Touch with a purpose. Use strategic placement with a connectedness goal in mind. Reach out and touch someone.

Following a seminar I presented for a middle school staff, a special education teacher approached me. "I liked your stuff on touch," she began. "Not enough of us on this staff touch, and I'm glad you encouraged that. But there's a hole in your touch material. There's a big empty spot that needs to be filled."

Intrigued by her comments, I encouraged her to continue.

"Some of our teachers do touch students appropriately. Not enough of them, but some do. Here's the hole. There is only one teacher in this school that lets students touch her. It's me. My students also have a need to touch. There are teachers who are comfortable touching students, but most are not comfortable *being* touched. My students like to hold my hand, stroke my hair, and put their arm around me. I let them. No other teacher in this building will allow it."

This special education teacher had learned the importance of giving her receiving. It's easy to give our giving, harder sometimes to give our receiving. Are there ways in which students can touch you? Are there ways they can give to you? Do you receive their giving?

Yes, with physical touch you have to respect boundaries—theirs and yours. Yes, it is important to touch in an appropriate context. Yes, it is important to do it only when others are around.

A second-grade teacher gives students a choice at the end of each day. "As you leave," she tells them, "you can give me a thumbs up, a high-five, or a hug." As they head out the door at the end of the day, they choose one of the three options and this Spirit Whisperer responds in kind.

A sixth-grade teacher encountered a student who often chose inappropriate behaviors and played the victim role. After four weeks of working with this child, the teacher was ready to call his parents and set up a conference, but before she took that step, in a last ditch effort she decided to implement a reach-out plan for the student. She scheduled sustained eye contact with him five times an hour and checked it off in her plan book as she achieved it. She purposefully smiled at him twice an hour and recorded it to make sure she followed through on her intention. She asked him his opinion about something once a day (e.g., "I'm thinking of buying a dog. What kind would you suggest?"). She made sure she had physical contact with him every day. She used proximity behavior and intentionally put herself in his vicinity regularly.

Within one week she began to see positive changes. Within a month she had built a positive relationship with this student, and the need to call the parents vanished.

A fourth-grade teacher schedules "greeting time" into his day. It's the first thing listed in his plan book every day. Greeting time consists of being by the classroom door and greeting each child as he or she enters. Each child receives a smile, eye contact, and a friendly comment upon entering this Spirit Whisperer's classroom.

A 15-year teaching veteran, a high school art teacher, found a letter in his school mailbox one day. In his school the mailboxes are in the office. If you've ever been in a high school office immediately following the final bell of the day, you're familiar with the scene. Students are coming and going. The phone is ringing. Students want to get permission slips, drop off assignments, use the phone, or pick up a hot lunch schedule. While "chaos" may be too strong a word to describe this portion of the school day, the minutes that follow the bell and precede the buses leaving are definitely filled with a flurry of scurry.

It was into this busy atmosphere that Charlie ventured one day and found the letter waiting in his mailbox. As students were busy doing their after school blitz on the office, he began to read its contents. "You probably don't remember me," it began, "but I had you for art a couple of years ago." Charlie turned quickly to the last page and checked the signature. He remembered this student. She had been in his class two semesters in a row when she was a senior.

"It has taken me a long time to write you," the letter went on. "I finally got up the courage to write. I wanted to tell you how important you have been to me and that you saved my life." Charlie felt his knees quiver a bit at the "saved my life" line and read on.

"I know a lot of people my age talk about suicide. Some are serious. Some are not. I was. A lot of things were bothering me and I didn't want to go on living any longer. So I created a plan. I knew when I was going to do it. I knew where. And I knew how. I had collected the material I needed and everything was in place. I was counting down the days.

"A few days before my plan was to be carried out, I was sitting in your class, looking bored I suppose. You came over to me and sat down beside me. You put your arm around me and asked if you could help. I mumbled a few things to you, enough so you knew I was struggling with important (to me) life issues. You stopped and listened to me. Then, with your arm still around me, you told me about a challenge you faced in your life and how you handled it. I remember you gave me a little hug for encouragement when class ended.

"I went home and thought about what you said. I rejected your solutions because they fit your situation more than they did mine. But I figured as long as there were people like you out there who lived their lives like they were glued together, then I could too. You seemed to like me so maybe I was likeable after all. I changed my mind that day about living. It hasn't been easy, but I am coping. Thank you for your support, your interest, and for saving my life. I just wanted you to know how important you have been to me."

Charlie was stunned. He left the office and drove home, where he shared the story with his wife. He said later that it was one of those drives where he didn't remember the intersections, didn't recall whether or not the lights were green. He was in a fog, shaken out of his comfort zone. "That letter shook me more than anything I can remember," he said. "It shook me right to the core."

When he was asked what it was about the incident that shook him up so much, Charlie remarked, "It wasn't the fact that she said I saved her life. Who knows about that for sure? It wasn't that I could have that much impact as a teacher. Every teacher knows their influence is far-reaching and can be dramatic. It wasn't that it was difficult to let her compliments in. I did okay with that. The thing that bothered me most, that really shook me, was that I don't even remember the incident. I remember her, but I don't know what day she was talking about. I don't even recall the conversation."

It didn't surprise me that Charlie couldn't remember the incident. He didn't remember it because he wasn't doing anything different that day than he did every other day of his teaching career. He was just busy being a professional educator. He was busy going about the process of spirit whispering.

Attempting to build a personal relationship with all the isolated, lonely students at your school would be an impossible task. There are so many of them. While it is not the teacher's job to be the support system for all these isolates, it is the teacher's job to create a support system.

To create that support system, Spirit Whisperers have turned to the cooperative learning technique to help them help students connect. It is one more way they activate the Principle of Oneness in their classrooms.

I'm not talking about putting kids into groups and telling them to work together. That's not cooperative learning. That's group work. Group work is different from cooperative learning and often creates divisiveness, separateness, and resentment.

Presented and structured unskillfully, group work can lead to alienation and distancing.

Many Spirit Whisperers are well-grounded in cooperative learning. They have participated in long-term, in-depth, skill-oriented training—45 hours or more, as taught in the Performance Learning Systems course, Achieving Student Outcomes Through Cooperative Learning™. They have learned to implement a model that teaches interpersonal skills as well as task skills. They have been taught techniques to purposefully structure positive interdependence into the design of the lesson so that students are encouraged to work together as well as to give and get support from one another. They have learned what interpersonal skills students need in order to function as effective team players and how to teach those skills. They have learned how to debrief lessons in ways that help students stay conscious of the choices they make during work time and how to set goals for the future. They have learned to stay out of groups as students work and to behave as interactionists rather than as interventionists. Because of their teachers' professional competence with the cooperative learning model, students experience unity, belonging, and friendship while simultaneously learning content.

Creating the "Our Classroom" feeling through the use of add-ons, group products, group goals, and other connectedness strategies is how Spirit Whisperers often begin the process of implementing the Principle of Oneness. Creating cooperative learning lessons that build positive interdependence adds another important layer to that process. Designing and following through with a reach-out plan for those students who appear especially isolated is another step Spirit Whisperers take to allow the Principle of Oneness to come alive in their classrooms.

One objection I've heard to the creation of oneness is that students will lose their individuality and that sameness will dominate uniqueness. "Why are you trying to make everyone the same?" critics question.

Do not confuse unity and connectedness with sameness. The sacrifice of individuality is not necessary in order to experience oneness. Both are desired. Both are valued. Unity and diversity can and do coexist in Spirit Whisperers' classrooms.

Diversity is on the increase in classrooms across the country. Widening mental and physical ability levels, a variety of cultural and ethnic origins, as well as individual student interests and preferences continue to stretch the boundaries and add ever-increasing amounts of diversity to the classroom mix.

The goal of the Principle of Oneness is to eliminate what divides people, not to eradicate what makes them different. Differences are valued and respected. Indeed, differences are celebrated in Spirit Whisperers' classrooms. It is divisiveness that needs to be eliminated from this equation, not differences.

Ghandi once said, "Our ability to reach unity in diversity will be the beauty and test of our civilization." An appropriate paraphrase would be, our ability to reach oneness in diversity will be the beauty and test of our educational system. Certainly, your ability to reach oneness in diversity in your classroom is a measure of who and what you are as a professional educator.

It's not agreement or absence of conflict that produce feelings of unity and the creation of an "Our Classroom" atmosphere. It's the acceptance of conflict that produces oneness. Accepting polarities on the continuum, acknowledging differing opinions, and honoring each other's experience—that's how the Principle of Oneness comes alive in classrooms.

Think of a close-knit family. Strong feelings of belonging exist within that family structure. Togetherness, unity, and oneness prevail because the family members are bonded. Yet, within that family there is variety. Some family members are bigger than others are. Some are older, some younger. Some have greater verbal skills than others do. Some like football, some horses. One is a vegetarian, one hunts deer. In spite of the differences, each family member is a part of the whole. In spite of the level of unity that family members feel, each is unique. Sameness and unity are not synonymous in healthy families and they're not synonymous in healthy classrooms either.

Creating oneness is not about turning black and white into gray. It's not about turning male and female into one androgynous being. Creating oneness is about finding a place in our classroom for black and a place for white. It's about making it okay to be male and okay to be female.

"This unity you talk about is unrealistic," a critic informed me. "There is no place where there isn't conflict, where there aren't disagreements. You'll never get everyone agreeing on anything. Unity is an impossible goal."

Ridding the classroom of conflict is not a goal of Spirit Whisperers. Holding conflict in a loving manner is. Appreciating conflict and respecting differing opinions is. Accepting conflict is.

Conflict brought into the heart does not split us into factions and destroy unity. Conflict experienced from a compassionate, open heart space does not lead to separation and distance. On the contrary, when conflict is welcomed, when differing opinions are accepted and seen as equally important, connectedness grows.

When conflict is explored in an arena of mutual respect, conflict is transcended. Students rise above the conflict and move to a place of acceptance, a place where they can honor the ideas, thoughts, feelings, and values of others even when they don't agree with them.

Make a safe place for diversity in your classroom. Celebrate the variety that exists within the unity. Create the "Our Classroom" feeling. When you do, you will create the breadth of connectedness that makes your classroom whole.

Conclusion

We are on the threshold of leaving behind the old way of teaching—the way based on right/wrong, competition, shame, fear, punishment, rescuing, judgement, demand for compliance, and obedience to outside authority. We are entering a new age—a time of awakening founded on trust, inner knowing, allowing, choice, personal power, responsibility, love, and unity.

A new teacher is emerging—one who is equipped to greet the evolving human consciousness that is showing up on our planet and in our students and classrooms. The old world, the old ways, the old curriculum are being slowly but surely left behind.

Enormous educational change is happening throughout the country. It is happening in the hearts and spirits of young people and their teachers. It is growing within individuals, within classrooms, and within schools. It is growing within you now or you wouldn't be reading this book.

Not everyone is conscious of the change that is taking place. Yet, everyone is feeling it on some level, including politicians, who have many constituents demanding increased high-stakes testing and accountability. Their protests are the dying gasp of the old way. Their noise is a desperate signal to retreat and circle the wagons in an effort to defend a time and place that is disintegrating—a final attempt to protect an era that is becoming history.

The old energy is rapidly giving way to the new. That new energy speaks to a child's spirit. Privately, day after day, Spirit Whisperers connect with their students, spirit to spirit. They are doing it without press conferences or attention-getting headlines. They are not making noise. Instead they are making a difference.

Spirit Whisperers are coming out of the closet—not with a bang and a clatter, but with an obvious and deliberate move toward teaching to the spirit. In growing numbers educators are walking across the bridge, moving out of the old ways into the invigorating climate of spirit whispering. The more they walk, the less they talk. And it's their walk that delivers their message.

Is it time for you to take another step toward becoming a Spirit Whisperer? No special place, no special material, no special time is needed. Where you are today is as fine as any place. "Bloom where you are planted," the saying goes. After all, it's where you are. The materials you have in front of you are as good as any others. The present moment is a time that will work as well as any future moment. And it is in the present moment that your responsibility lies.

There is no obligation in spirit whispering—only opportunity. All you need do is what you must do anyway—make choices. What choices you make create and define who and what you are as a professional educator.

There is no order to the steps involved in becoming a Spirit Whisperer. There is nothing you have to do first. Just step. That step will reveal the step that comes next. You will know it by listening to the spirit that moves within you. Trust yourself. You know. And you know that you know. Politicians don't have your answers. State departments of education don't have your answers. Grade level guides and textbook companies don't have your answers. College professors don't have your answers, nor does the teacher across the hall or your union building representative. Your answers come from within. Trust that inner voice.

Your journey into spirit whispering doesn't have much to do with anyone else. It's mostly about you. It's about your thoughts, beliefs, feelings, and actions. It's about how you choose to be and how you choose to create yourself in response to where you find yourself now.

This book cannot tell you your way. The best it can do is remind you of what you already know. It can bring to awareness what you have forgotten or ignored, but it cannot determine your truth. That is for you alone to decide.

ABOUT THE AUTHOR

Chick Moorman

C hick Moorman is the director of the Institute for Personal Power, a consulting firm dedicated to providing high quality professional development activities for educators and parents.

He is a former classroom teacher with over 35 years of experience in the field of education. His mission is to help people experience a greater sense of personal power in their lives so they can in turn empower others.

Chick conducts full-day workshops and seminars for school districts and parent groups. He also delivers keynote addresses for local, state, and national conferences.

He is available for the following topic areas:

FOR EDUCATORS

- Achievement Motivation and Behavior Management through Effective Teacher Talk
- Teaching Respect and Responsibility
- Improving Student Self-Esteem
- Stamping Out Learned Helplessness
- Cooperative Learning
- Celebrate the Spirit Whisperers
- Dealing with Reluctant Learners

FOR PARENTS

- Parent Talk: Words That Empower, Words That Wound
- Raising Your Child's Self-Esteem
- Empowered Parenting
- Building Family Solidarity
- Developing Positive Attitudes in Children

If you would like more information about these programs or would like to discuss a possible training or speaking date, please contact:

The Institute for Personal Power
P.O. Box 547
Merrill, MI 48637
Telephone: 1 (877) 360-1477
Fax: (517) 643-5156
E-mail: ipp57@aol.com
Web site: www.chickmoorman.com

Other Products by Chick Moorman

TEACHER TALK: WHAT IT REALLY MEANS

Chick Moorman and Nancy Weber
(paperback) $13.00

This book is about teachers' talk—the comments, questions, commands, and suggestions that teachers direct at students every day. It explores the way teachers talk to children and exposes the underlying "silent messages" that accompany their spoken words.

Eighty percent of all talking in classrooms is done by teachers. Sometimes that talk is lecture. Other times it involves giving directions, reprimanding, reminding, praising, suggesting, discussing, motivating, or explaining. As a teacher, your choice of words and your language selections are critical to the self-esteem, the academic success, and the healthy mental and emotional development of your students. There is an undeniable link between the words you speak and the attitudes and outcomes students create in their lives. By selecting words and phrases intentionally; by altering your present language; by adding to or taking away from your common utterances you can empower your students and enhance their learning. *Teacher Talk: What It Really Means* will help you do just that.

OUR CLASSROOM: WE CAN LEARN TOGETHER

Chick Moorman and Dee Dishon
(hardcover) $20.00

This book will help K-6 teachers create a classroom environment where discipline problems are less likely to occur and where students are less likely to activate the new three R's: Resistance, Reluctance, and Resentment. It will show you how to build an atmosphere of togetherness and cooperation as it focuses on activities and strategies that foster notions of belonging, interdependence, and mutual respect.

TALK SENSE TO YOURSELF: THE LANGUAGE OF PERSONAL POWER

Chick Moorman
(paperback) $13.00

There is a connection between the words you use, the beliefs you hold, and the actions you take. This book explores that connection and shows you how you can purposefully select language that creates within you the programming necessary to change the quality and direction of your life.

Contained within the book is a series of words, phrases, and ways of speaking that will increase your sense of personal power. *Talk Sense to Yourself: The Language of Personal Power* will help you structure your language patterns to put more choice and possibility in your life. You will become more self-confident, improve your self-esteem, and learn how to talk sense to yourself.

WHERE THE HEART IS: STORIES OF HOME AND FAMILY

Chick Moorman and 72 Contributing Authors
(paperback) $15.00

A treasury of inspirational stories about home and family to help you celebrate family strength, love, tolerance, hope, and commitment. Delight in what is possible with loving, caring family members. Seventy-two authors dedicated to the belief that family matters. Ninety stories to nourish your soul.

PARENT TALK:
WORDS THAT EMPOWER, WORDS THAT WOUND

Chick Moorman
(hardcover) $25.00

This book is about how parents talk to their children. It reveals verbal communication that scolds, shames, and criticizes, as well as words that praise, nurture, and empower children. By altering your present language—by adding or taking away from your parent talk—you can empower your children and enhance their effectiveness as capable, responsible, and caring human beings.

Learn how to speak in ways that reduce family conflict, build family solidarity, demonstrate listening, build trust and caring, and help children develop positive core beliefs. This is a skill-based book that will help you give your children opportunities to practice responsibility and learn from their experiences.

PARENT TALK FOCUS CARDS

Chick Moorman
(card deck) $10.00

A 50-piece card deck that summarizes The Parent Talk System concepts. The front of each card displays a popular and effective Parent Talk phrase. The reverse side contains a brief explanation of the concept and additional examples. Ideal for posting on your refrigerator or dash board as gentle reminders.

REDUCING FAMILY CONFLICT THROUGH EFFECTIVE PARENT TALK

Chick Moorman
(video) $30.00

This video reveals the importance of Parent Talk and tells how our words can empower or wound our children. Ways of speaking to and with children that reduce family conflict are covered. Learn how to reduce power struggles while encouraging mutual respect with the Parent Talk skills presented on this video. 60 minutes.

The Parent Talk System:
Facilitator's Manual, The Language
of Response-able Parenting
Chick Moorman, Sarah Knapp, and Judith Minton
(manual) $300.00

This 120-page manual is designed to help trainers deliver the 12-hour Parent Talk System seminar to interested parents. A step-by-step explanation of each session is provided with videos, transparencies, and directions. To be used in conjunction with a participant workbook.

To order any of these materials call **1 (877) 360-1477** or send the order form below to **Personal Power Press, P.O. Box 547, Merrill, MI 48637**.

PRODUCT ORDER FORM

TITLE	QUANTITY	PRICE
_____	_____	_____
_____	_____	_____
_____	_____	_____
_____	_____	_____
_____	_____	_____

MI residents add 6% sales tax   _____

Shipping & Handling   _____

Total enclosed   [   ]

PLEASE ADD THE FOLLOWING SHIPPING AND HANDLING CHARGES:

| $0 - $15.00 | $3.75 | $30.01 - $50.00 | $5.75 |
| $15.01 - $30.00 | $4.75 | $50.01 & up | 10% of total order |

CANADA: 20% of total order. US funds only, please.

NAME _____

ADDRESS _____

CITY _____ STATE _____ ZIP _____

PHONE NUMBER _____

PERFORMANCE LEARNING SYSTEMS

Performance Learning Systems

GRADUATE COURSES

Performance Learning Systems offers graduate courses that teach educators strategies and techniques consistent with the principles of spirit whispering. They pride themselves on offering skill-oriented courses throughout the United States, Canada, and Australia that are research-based. The following PLS courses address the Spirit Whisperer concept.

SUCCESSFUL TEACHING FOR ACCEPTANCE OF RESPONSIBILITY™

A practical course that provides strategies for modeling and teaching responsible student behaviors. Encourage responsibility by helping students develop an inner sense of personal power. Learn how to give students models of expectations, accountability, organization, goal setting, internal standards, and more. Obtain the tools and language that can eliminate learned helplessness and other irresponsible behavior.

The Principles of Personal Responsibility, Personal Power, and Conscious Creation are covered extensively in the course, as is the concept of debriefing.

ACHIEVING STUDENT OUTCOMES THROUGH COOPERATIVE LEARNING™

Demonstrates effective techniques for working with students in groups. Teachers learn how to weave students' mastery of a particular subject with the development and use of lifelong interpersonal and questioning skills.

Suspended judgment, debriefing, empowering groups, and the Principle of Oneness are Spirit Whisperer concepts taught in this course.

PURPOSEFUL LEARNING THROUGH MULTIPLE INTELLIGENCES™

Introduces Howard Gardner's research on intelligence and shows educators how to apply and implement multiple intelligences in the classroom.

PRIDE™
(PROFESSIONAL REFINEMENTS IN DEVELOPING EFFECTIVENESS)

Introduces teachers to advanced questioning skills and strategies and gives them the opportunity to master those skills and strategies. The course covers important nonverbal communication skills and methods to manage classroom disruptions and improve teacher presentations.

PROJECT TEACH™
(TEACHER EFFECTIVENESS AND CLASSROOM HANDLING)

Provides strategies for immediately successful classroom management. This course teaches verbal skills and strategies to help participants master positive communication and team-building skills.

For further information on these and other graduate courses offered by **Performance Learning Systems** contact:

PLS
466 Old Hook Road
Emerson, NJ 07630
Telephone: 1 (800) 526-4630
E-mail: pls@aol.com
Web site: www.pls-ed.com